Free to Be

Lessons in Liberty
For the American Christian

B. Kay Coulter

xulon PRESS

Copyright © 2004 by B. Kay Coulter

Free To Be
by B. Kay Coulter

Printed in the United States of America

ISBN 1-594673-84-5

All rights reserved by the author. The contents and views expressed in this book are solely those of the author and are not necessarily those of Xulon Press, Inc. The author guarantees this book is original and does not infringe upon any laws or rights, and that this book is not libelous, plagiarized or in any other way illegal. If any portion of this book is fictitious, the author guarantees it does not represent any real event or person in a way that could be deemed libelous. No part of this book may be reproduced in any form without the permission of the author.

Unless otherwise indicated, Bible quotations are taken from the New International Version. Copyright © 1973, 1978, 1984 by Holman Bible Publishers, Nashville, TN.

Unless otherwise indicated, word definitions are taken from the dictionary software WordWeb 2.2 Freeware Version. Copyright © Antony Lewis 2003.

fr. Kay Coulter
b. 26:3

Acknowledgments

First of all, I must acknowledge the guidance of the Holy Spirit as I wrote these pages. If it were not for God's leading that compelled me to write, I would surely falter in communicating to readers the lessons I have learned in the forty plus years I have been a Christian. Secondly, I wish to acknowledge my dear friend, ministry partner, and professional editor Janet Crews for performing her service in editing this book with her usual "grammar police" intensity. I would also like to acknowledge my friend Joann Northen, who I have invited to contribute as a guest writer for the lesson on blindness. It is my prayer that this book will prove to be thought provoking and challenging to readers, inspiring all to be *free to be* all God wants us to be.

B. Kay Coulter

Table of Contents

Introduction xi

Day 1
    Fly Like an Eagle 15

Day 2
    Toss It Out 21

Day 3
    No Limits 25

Day 4
    Freedom Through Forgiveness 29

Day 5
    Free Speech 35

Day 6
    Free from Anxiety 39

Day 7
    Free to Live Purposefully 43

Day 8
    Trapped by Our Words 49

Day 9
    Freed from Sin – Slaves to Righteousness 55

Day 10
    Free from Death 59

Day 11
    Free from Darkness 65

Day 12
    Free from Blindness 69

Day 13
    Freed from the Bondage of the Past 77

Day 14
    Freedom from Thirst 83

Day 15
    Liberty is Not License 89

Day 16
    Substitute or Satisfaction 93

Day 17
    Free to Worship 97

Day 18
    Free from Prejudice 101

Day 19
    Free from Greed 107

Day 20
    Free from Condemnation 111

Day 21
    Free from Self-righteousness 117

Day 22
    Free to Serve 123

Day 23
    Free to Love 129

Day 24
    Free from Legalism 135

Day 25
    The Power Released 141

Day 26
> Escape!...147

Day 27
> Free from Falsehood.............................151

Day 28
> Free from Pride....................................157

Day 29
> Things From Which We Cannot Be Free 163

Day 30
> Grace—Free But Not Cheap................................169

Introduction

OPERATION IRAQI FREEDOM!— read the headlines of the newspapers all across the country in March of 2003. At that time the United States had joined with allied forces from other countries to oust the heinous dictator Saddam Hussein from his country and to secure freedom for millions of Iraqis who have suffered greatly under his rule. There is not a day that passes that we do not see and hear on the media news programs the horrors of this war. We have gained a measure of success, as Hussein has been captured, but the job is not finished. We are trying to introduce the ideals of democratic rule to the Iraqi people, so they can be "free" and have their individual rights protected.

As I have observed this drama unfold, I have thought a lot about freedom and what it means from a Biblical perspective. Though I am sure that the lives of Iraqis (who are primarily Muslims) will be improved in a democratic "free" society, I cannot help but wonder if we should do more. As a Christian nation (at least many in the world see us that way), I believe we are not bringing real freedom to the people until we bring them the Gospel. It is my prayer that the door to missionary activity will open, and millions of Iraqis will turn from a dead religion to the Christian message of redemption and resurrection that only comes through Jesus Christ. This is my prayer for millions of Americans as well, for there are still many who do not understand the real meaning of freedom.

This book is about real freedom. It is not a book of pat answers or stated formulas that lead to freedom but rather it is a guide to serve you as you embark on a journey alongside a loving God, encountering His truths, and incorporating those truths into your life. The format is designed to be a daily devotional, with Scripture references, teaching, and words upon which to meditate. In my book *Victim/Victor: It's Your Choice,* I go into great detail explaining the "how" of getting free. This devotional guide is not a "how-to" book in that sense but rather emphasizes the many Scriptures that have to do with freedom—release from captivity, deliverance, relief, etc. It is my prayer that the reader will ruminate on these Scriptures, and will come to appreciate the freedom that comes to those who have committed their lives to Christ.

Though the book is in a daily devotional format, please do not feel restricted. It is okay to take several days to meditate on a lesson, for sometimes that is how God speaks to us. Though there are thirty devotionals, you do not have to finish in thirty days. This is not a test!

After having been in ministry for over twenty years and having counseled many, I have concluded that many Christians really do not understand the freedom we have in Christ. Many are in bondage to fear, to bad habits, to destructive attitudes and behaviors, and to false teaching within the church. The Apostle Paul, in writing to the Galatian Christians in regard to false teaching concerning the Law, states it this way: "It is for freedom that Christ has set us free. Stand firm, then, and do not let yourselves be burdened again by a yoke of slavery" (Galatians 5:1). Many things can enslave us, but we have the choice of whether or not we allow ourselves to be enslaved. So, let us begin our journey to freedom, where truth leads the way: "Then you will know the truth, and the truth will set you free" (John 8:32).

Day 1

Fly Like an Eagle

From the Dictionary

Free: Verb – Grant freedom to; free from confinement.

From the Word

Isaiah 40:28-31

> Do you not know? Have you not heard? The LORD is the everlasting God, the Creator of the ends of the earth. He will not grow tired or weary, and his understanding no one can fathom. He gives strength to the weary and increases the power of the weak. Even youths grow tired and weary, and young men stumble and fall; but those who hope in the LORD will renew their strength. They will soar on wings like eagles; they will run and not grow weary, they will walk and not be faint.

Also read Isaiah 55:9; Ecclesiastes 3:11

How can we soar like an eagle when we are constrained by earthbound thinking? Perhaps we need to think like a bird? Does the thought of soaring above the crowd appeal to you? Or would you like to soar above life's painful circumstances? When I was a little girl, I wished that I were a bird. I even dreamed about it a lot. In my dreams I would fly over the schoolyard of the country school that I attended.

All the children would look up at me and express their wonder at my ability. Oh, what a view I had—a bird's-eye view, if you please!

What is even better than a bird's-eye view? I call it a God's eye-view. A God's-eye view means getting God's perspective on my circumstances. Often, when my faith is slipping, my inclination as a Christian is to look up—up to Heaven, making my pleas to God for help. This gives me perspective on my situation.

There have been times in my life when I have had the awesome privilege of getting God's perspective on my circumstances. I am reminded of the times that I have climbed (or ridden) to the top of a mountain and God has opened my eyes to His greatness. There is something about the view from atop a mountain or hill that changes our perspective—on problems, on circumstances, on God's work, on life in general. Looking up to the hills from the valley below raises my eyes toward the sky. This perspective reminds me of God's omnipotence and vastness, as well as my insignificance. Yet at the same time, I come to appreciate God's grace even more, because He does not treat me as being insignificant. The Psalmist expresses this wonder in Psalm 8:4 (ASV): "When I consider thy heavens, the work of thy fingers, The moon and the stars, which thou hast ordained; What is man, that thou art mindful of him?"

One of my most significant memories of "from-the-mountain-viewing" is when my husband and I were visiting Switzerland in 1993. As part of our tour we went by train and air-tram up to the peak of Stanser Horn Mountain in the Alps. It was truly a "holy wow" kind of experience for me. At first we were with a group, then John and I wandered around to another side of the mountain (a sidewalk with a rail was provided!). Then I went a little farther by myself. I reached a vantage point where I could view the city of Lucerne and the lake that is in the middle of the it. What a view! Then as I stood admiring the view (both God-made and man-made), I noticed a military jet flying *below* me! To think—I was standing in a place so high that I was above the path of the jet! Incredible! My response was to burst forth in song! I sang "How Majestic Is Your Name," a song I used often in my concerts. The song lifted me up even higher as I expressed the deep things of my heart, which is so often true in using music to communicate. It came very naturally to me since it seemed as if I were closer to Heaven at 10,000 feet above sea level. It was an experience of great spiritual significance. God was teaching me about His ability to view my life and circumstances from a vantage point that enabled Him to see "the big picture." It helped me realize that I could have the same perspective if I would but "lift my eyes to the hills"—take in the beautiful view of my Lord. Problems, circumstances, trials all became minuscule in comparison to God's power.

The lesson learned atop that mountain still serves me today and is reinforced every time I sing with a sincere heart. I believe God gave me this experience not just for my enlightenment but also to prepare me for the valley times I would experience in the future. I can still go to Stanser Horn in my mind, recall the view, my response, and God's speaking to my heart. I am then lifted up in my spirit and soar like an eagle—rising above the mundane and dwelling on the miraculous.

Questions to Ponder

Question 1: Can you think of a time when God lifted you up, helping you rise above difficulties?

Question 2: In what ways are you earthbound in your thinking? What grabs your interest? What passions consume you?

Question 3: How can you change your perspective on your current circumstances?

Memorize

Isaiah 40:31 (NIV)

"But those who hope in the LORD will renew their strength. They will soar on wings like eagles; they will run and not grow weary, they will walk and not be faint."

NOTES

Day 2

Toss It Out

From the Dictionary

Free: Verb – Relieve from.

From the Word

Hebrews 13:5 (NIV)

> Keep your lives free from the love of money and be content with what you have, because God has said, "Never will I leave you; never will I forsake you.

Also read Matthew 6:19-21; Luke 12:15

To get rid of something is to free one from its presence. In getting rid of something, we get relief. I think of the times when I have been very industrious and decided to clean out a closet. There are several closets in my house that do not hold clothing but rather are filled (sometimes to overflowing) with all kinds of things I decided at the time to keep. After keeping these things for several years, though, I sometimes forget why I am keeping them and have to make some tough decisions: What to keep? What to give away? What to throw away? The clutter is about to overtake me! So, with determination, I tackle the task. It's amazing how many things I can actually throw away! After working hard and getting the closet back into order, there is a great sense of satisfaction and accomplishment.

I think that sometimes life is a lot like a cluttered closet. I find that I need to take the time to examine my attitudes, my passions, and my priorities. Certainly, I will discover some things that need to be thrown out—like old habits of being critical and judgmental; or compulsions that take too much of my focus (like computer games!); or too much time and money spent on my outward appearance and not enough spent on inner beauty. When these things are turned over to God, He releases me (frees me) to become engaged in His work. The clutter is gone from my mind and I can become more effective in witnessing and ministering to others.

I also find that when I "release" my closet from much of its clutter, I am reminded that my life does not consist in "things" but rather in my relationship with the Father.

Questions to Ponder

Question 1: What are some things (attitudes, habits, etc.) that are cluttering your mind?

Question 2: Calculate approximately how much time you are spending on unnecessary activities.

Question 3: Ask God to show you what to throw out, what to keep, and what to give away. List these.

Memorize

2 Corinthians 10:5 (NIV)

> **"We demolish arguments and every pretension that sets itself up against the knowledge of God, and we take captive every thought to make it obedient to Christ."**

NOTES

Day 3

No Limits

From the Dictionary

Free: Verb – Grant relief or an exemption from a rule or requirement to.

From the Word

Exodus 21:2-3 (NIV)

> If you buy a Hebrew servant, he is to serve you for six years. But **in the seventh year, he shall go free,** without paying anything. (emphasis mine)

Also read Leviticus 25:10; Exodus 20:11; Romans 8:20-21

Under God's laws in the Old Testament, Jews who were bought as slaves were to serve six years, then in the seventh year, go free. The Life Application Bible Notes gives us a reason for this seventh-year freedom: "But Hebrew slaves were treated as humans, not property, and were allowed to work their way to freedom."

In the New Testament we are told how Christ's work of sacrifice on the cross has secured our freedom from slavery to our earthly bodies and earthly ways. God loves and treats us like humans who have need of a Savior. He knows we cannot work our way to Heaven, so He has provided the way for our freedom. We, as God's children, are bound to servitude as long we are in the flesh (subject to temptation, hostility, abuse, etc.). Christ, however, has purchased our freedom, and when death comes, we are free to enter Heaven by God's grace. We will be free of those things that bind us and limit us because of our earthly bodies and because of sin in the world.

I think of a friend who recently passed away—his name was Harry. He was bound by physical limitations but still served God faithfully as best he could. He was about 83 and had lived a long life of service to God. He loved God and His Word, and Harry loved sharing the Gospel with others. The last few years of his life were spent in and out of the hospital. His body was bent by back surgery and Parkinson's Disease. Much of the time he was confined to a wheelchair, but he rarely complained. He became a prisoner of his own body when it stopped functioning normally, yet he was free in his mind, because he had placed his trust in Jesus Christ. He accepted his captivity but did not dwell on it. He just continued to serve the Lord as he had opportunity, being a great prayer warrior and encourager. When he died, he was freed from his bent body and the confining wheel chair. He went to Heaven, where today he is "standing tall." Heaven is the ultimate destination of freedom for all who place our trust in Jesus. We will someday join those like Harry and stand before a loving and just God. We will give to God an account of our work on earth, and to those who have been faithful, He will say, "Well done, thou good and faithful servant" (Matthew 25:21).

Questions to Ponder

Question1: Are you faithful in your service, in spite of limitations?

Question 2: Do you have the assurance that Christ is your

Savior and you have the promise of eternal life?

Memorize

Romans 5:8 (NIV)

"But God demonstrates his own love for us in this: While we were still sinners, Christ died for us."

NOTES

Day 4

Freedom through Forgiveness

From the Dictionary

Free: Adjective – Not held in servitude.

From the Word

Exodus 6:6 (NIV)

> I am the LORD, and I will bring you out from under the yoke of the Egyptians. I will free you from being slaves to them, and I will redeem you with an outstretched arm and with mighty acts of judgment.

Also read Matthew 5:23-24; Matthew 6:12-15; 2 Corinthians 5:17-18.

"I am the LORD"— God identified Himself as the great **I AM** to Moses. It was He who made the promise to deliver the Hebrews from slavery. No one else had the power to deliver them. Sin is like the bondage of the ancient Jewish people in Egypt. Theirs was a forced yoke of slavery imposed upon them. They had no control over their circumstances.

There are some people who try to enslave us by imposing their wills on us; some circumstances over which we have no control are:

    (a. Oppression by others

(b. Abuse
(c. Disabilities, etc.

Even if we are victims, however, we can be free in our minds by forgiving those who hurt us. Without forgiveness, we place ourselves in bondage to the one who abused us. We must trust God to bring to judgment those who would hurt us. He will and He does. Freedom comes as we are reconciled to God and to others. We can be free to forgive others as we realize that God has forgiven us. Remember the model prayer by Jesus? Matthew 6:12 (NIV) records it for us: "Forgive us our debts, as we also have forgiven our debtors."

And James tells us: "Therefore confess your sins to each other and pray for each other so that you may be healed" (James 5:16).

"So that you may be healed" stands out to me in this last verse. Many victims are seeking to be healed, but they are clueless when it comes to God's antidotes for the emotional toxins that invade their souls. We have in this verse a most important principle—that of confessing our sins to one another. Wow! Just think of the implications if Christians took this principle seriously. If we would put into practice this simple command, we could watch the river of forgiveness flow throughout the Body of Christ. People would be freed from holding grudges, from engaging in angry outbursts, and from manipulating others for self-serving purposes. The result would be unity in the Body and joy in the Lord.

I had an experience years ago when my ability to forgive was challenged. I remember in great detail how I was hurt, the time that I spent in depression, and ultimately coming to the Lord for healing. At that time I was leading a women's Bible study group in my church (not teaching, but facilitating). It was my responsibility to promote the study, to sign up teachers on various topics, and to lead prayer and discussion time. I took my responsibility seriously and really felt I was in the center of God's will. The years I spent in this leadership position were a great training ground for life. At this time in my life, though, I did not have a lot of self-confidence and was particularly sensitive to criticism. I was generally well-liked, however, so I really did not consider that there might be those in the group who would oppose me. As it happened, there were two women in the group who decided I wasn't "Spirit-led" in my leadership, so they took it upon themselves to correct me. They accused me of quenching the Holy Spirit, but other than that they were rather vague in pointing out what it was I was doing wrong. I was baffled as to what I could be doing wrong and hurt in the way these two ladies went about confronting me and turning others against me. The situation got out of hand and after several weeks of soul-searching, I decided it would be best if I resigned. I felt I had been unjustly accused and was the victim of "spiritual abuse."

The criticism resulted in my going into a months-long depression, causing me to question my relationship with God and His will for me. I had felt I was doing God's will in leading the group, but I was not mature enough to be objective and know how to receive criticism. It was some time before I actively participated in church functions again. The wound went deeply into my heart and for a time I had to struggle with whether or not I could forgive these women who had taken away my ministry (or so it seemed at the time). I was so afraid I would mess up again, so I held back from contributing any service. The day came, however, with the help of my husband and a friend who stood by me that I was able to get a clearer picture of the whole incident. As I came to this realization, I was able to forgive the women. It was after I had forgiven them (though they did not come to me asking for forgiveness until two years later) that I became free to minister again in the ways in which God had called me.

Questions to Ponder

Question 1: To whom are you looking to save you?

Question 2: Is there someone in your past who you need to forgive? Confess and repent so the love of God can flow through you, enabling you to forgive. Therein is great freedom.

Question 3: Is there someone from whom you need forgiveness?

Memorize

Ephesians 4:31-32 (NIV)

"Get rid of all bitterness, rage and anger, brawling and slander, along with every form of malice. Be kind and compassionate to one another, forgiving each other, just as in Christ God forgave you."

Free To Be

NOTES

Day 5

Free Speech

From the Dictionary

License: Noun – Freedom to deviate deliberately from normally applicable rules or practices (especially in behavior or speech).

From the Word

Romans 6:15-22

> I put this in human terms because you are weak in your natural selves. Just as you used to offer the parts of your body in slavery to impurity and to ever-increasing wickedness, so now offer them in slavery to righteousness leading to holiness. When you were slaves to sin, you were free from the control of righteousness. What benefit did you reap at that time from the things you are now ashamed of? Those things result in death! But now that you have been set free from sin and have become slaves to God, the benefit you reap leads to holiness, and the result is eternal life.

Also read Psalm 119:32, 45

In America there seems to be this notion that because we live in a "free" nation, we as individuals are free to do anything we please. Think of the abuses of the freedom of speech! People fight to exercise this freedom in all kinds of evil and corrupt speech. Has this resulted in good for our society? I think not. Because this one "right" is in our Constitution, many perverse interpretations have arisen in the entertainment industry and the media, including libelous speech, pornography, and crude and blasphemous language.

It seems to me that all this is not freedom, but rather bondage—bondage to the baseness of human nature. God has said that true freedom comes to those who obey Him. He has clearly communicated to us, via the Bible, high standards for living. If we live within the boundaries of His Word, we are indeed free. If we apply this principle to our speech, for instance, we will avoid cursing, crudity, blasphemy, etc. Instead of resorting to the lowest kind of communication, we should speak in such a way as to be helpful to others.

One time I saw an illustration given by a speaker for our memory verse today: Ephesians 4:29. She was speaking to a group of children and wanted to help them understand the importance of the words they spoke. As she talked, she began to build a tower of wooden blocks. She built it high enough for everyone to see. Then she asked a child from the audience to come and assist her. She said the building blocks were like the words we spoke. As long as we spoke encouraging words, we would be "building up" others, but negative words of criticism and complaining would have the opposite effect. At that point, she asked her assistant to knock down the tower of blocks (which he did with glee, I might add!). The children understood the lesson that we have power in the words that we speak—for good or for evil. It was a powerful lesson for me as well as the children. I desire to be one who builds up others and I rejoice when I see good come from my words.

If we live according to God's Word, we will live fruitful, satisfying lives, filled with His joy, and we will be good citizens who try to do what's best for our society. Is this not the kind of freedom we should pursue and protect? True freedom comes through obedience.

Questions to Ponder

Question 1: In what ways do you think disobedience is slavery?

Question 2: In what ways do you think obedience leads to freedom?

Question 3: In examining your heart, do you find areas of disobedience, resulting in your own captivity?

Memorize

Ephesians 4:29 (NIV)

> **"Do not let any unwholesome talk come out of your mouths, but only what is helpful for building others up according to their needs, that it may benefit those who listen."**

NOTES

Day 6

Free from Anxiety

From the Dictionary

Anguish: Noun – An agonizing pain of the body or mind; torment.

From the Word

Romans 7:21-25

> So I find this law at work: When I want to do good, evil is right there with me. For in my inner being I delight in God's law; but I see another law at work in the members of my body, waging war against the law of my mind and making me a prisoner of the law of sin at work within my members. What a wretched man I am! Who will rescue me from this body of death? Thanks be to God—through Jesus Christ our Lord!

Also read Psalm 118:5; Luke 13:12-13

In Romans 7 Paul speaks of his inner anguish—the torment of the mind that comes at times to the Christian who has to live *in* the world but not be *of* the world. Satan wants to draw us away from God, and he uses all the tools at his disposal. The anguish of mind comes when we must make choices about temptation. The flesh is at war with the spirit, and the only relief is when we allow God's Spirit, through Jesus, to conquer the flesh.

The crippled woman in Luke 13 experienced a different kind of anguish. For eighteen long years she had been forced by her condition to bend over. The Bible says that Satan had crippled the woman by an evil spirit. Think of it! She always had to look down! Surely, this must have led to depression. Oh, the anguish she must have suffered in her mind as well as her body. She had such a limited view of life. How many of us suffer anguish of mind because of our limited views? It is easy to be a pessimist when our circumstances do not go as we would like.

I have just experienced a taste of this kind of anguish. I have a chronic pain problem, causing me to suffer with periodic attacks on my digestive system. Most of the time it is just a nuisance, but occasionally I experience a very painful episode. This was the case the other night, as I awoke with intense abdominal pain and sickness. I awoke my husband because I felt like I might faint if I tried to get up to take medicine. He tended to me, helping me through the worst of it. The physical symptoms were difficult to deal with but the mental anguish was worse. Questions began going through my head, causing me to wonder if I would be able to go in just a few weeks on a planned mission trip to Canada. Would I have to cancel? Would I be able to handle the travel? Would I be able to eat the food without triggering another attack? I also experienced turmoil in my mind when I thought of other people who would be counting on me—my friend who would be traveling with me; the leaders in charge of the mission; my husband who might have to decide not to let me go. Indeed, mine was an anguished mind as I pondered the possibilities.

Thankfully, I did not stay in this state of anguish long. Just the morning before I had read the passages for this day's study, and God brought these words to my mind. As a result, I thought about what the cure is for "anguish syndrome." I was prompted by the Holy Spirit to turn over to God all my cares—all those worries and "what ifs"—about my trip and my physical condition. When I did, I began to experience His peace—the peace that passes all understanding. I could then agree with the Psalmist, "In my anguish I cried to the Lord, and he answered by setting me free."

Questions to Ponder

1. *Can you recall a time when you were in anguish about an event, a relationship, a circumstance?*

2. *Did God bring to mind scriptures that addressed your situation?*

3. *Have you experienced God's peace in times of trouble and anxiety? Write down one or two experiences, remembering to thank God for caring for you.*

Memorize

Matthew 6:33-34 (NIV)

"But seek first his kingdom and his righteousness, and all these things will be given to you as well. Therefore do not worry about tomorrow, for tomorrow will worry about itself. Each day has enough trouble of its own."

NOTES

Day 7

Freedom to Live Purposefully

From the Dictionary

Plumbline: Noun – A cord from which a metal weight is suspended pointing directly to the earth's center of gravity; used to determine the vertical from a given point.

From the Word

Isaiah 61:1: (NIV)

> The Spirit of the Sovereign LORD is on me, because the LORD has anointed me to preach good news to the poor. He has sent me to bind up the broken-hearted, to proclaim freedom for the captives and release from darkness for the prisoners….

Also read Isaiah 61, Philippians 1:21, and Philippians 3.

When Jesus was teaching in the synagogue at Nazareth, He read aloud from the above passage in Isaiah, applying it to Himself. I believe that Jesus' purpose on the earth is encapsulated in this passsage. Jesus had a very clear picture of His purpose in laying aside the glory of Heaven and submitting to the Father's plan of redemption for mankind. His purpose was to:
- Preach good news to the poor.
- Proclaim freedom for the prisoners.
- Recover sight to the blind.

43

- Release the oppressed.
- Proclaim the year of God's favor.

We as followers of Christ still have the privilege and responsibility to carry out Jesus' purpose on earth. After the crucifixion and resurrection, He commissioned His followers to continue proclaiming His message and then He ascended into Heaven. This remains as our purpose today. Our very purpose for living can be defined by Jesus' purpose. As long as God allows His Church to remain, our purpose is to carry out the ministry that our Lord and Savior began. First we must lay aside selfish pursuits, look to God for guidance, and purposefully serve Him as we minister the gospel to others.

It is a wonderful thing to know our purpose for living—to be able to live life confidently in such a way that pleases the Father and positively impacts the world around us. Paul stated it this way in Philippians 1:21: "For me to live is Christ, and to die is gain." At the end of his life, Paul was still faithful in carrying out his goals. He encouraged the early Christians to press on, just as he did: "I press on to take hold of that for which Christ Jesus took hold of me" (Philippians 3:12 NIV).

Many in today's world are chasing after counterfeit happiness, seeking to have meaning in their lives. God's purposes, as exhibited by Christ, can serve as a plumbline by which to measure our lives. Sometimes this means adjustments in our thinking.

When I started out in ministry, I was primarily a singer. For a number of years and in numerous places, I was called upon to testify of God's greatness and to witness through the gift of song. God spoke to me about committing my voice to Him when I was just sixteen. I had no reason to believe I would ever have a different kind of ministry than singing. God, however, broadened the scope of my ministry by teaming me up with a friend, and gradually I found myself speaking as well as singing. So the ministry vehicle began to change. Now, in the last few years, I have begun to write, and God has shown me that this will be my primary vehicle for ministry. So I see that I have gone through a metamorphosis—from singer to speaker to writer. This was no easy task, and it required quite a lot of adjustments along the way. However, I find myself asking, "Am I still living according to God's purposes?" The answer to that question is affirmative, as long as I measure all I do by His plumbline. His purposes have not changed, and my assignment to be a communicator has not changed, but God has stretched and grown me to be willing to communicate His message in different ways. No matter the vehicle, I am still preaching good news to the poor, proclaiming freedom for the prisoners, helping people to see (truth), relieving the oppressed, and proclaiming the year of God's favor (the coming of Jesus).

Questions to Ponder

Question 1: Do you have a sense of purpose in living your life? Write down what you think this is.

Question 2. Are you being obedient to follow God's purposes for you, or have you veered off course?

Question 3: What measure do you use for success?

Memorize

Philippians 3:12-14 (NIV)

> **Not that I have already obtained all this, or have already been made perfect, but I press on to take hold of that for which Christ Jesus took hold of me. Brothers, I do not consider myself yet to have taken hold of it. But one thing I do: Forgetting**

what is behind and straining toward what is ahead, I press on toward the goal to win the prize for which God has called me heavenward in Christ Jesus.

NOTES

Day 8

Trapped by our Words

From the Dictionary

Word: Noun – An angry dispute,
[as in "have words" with someone].

From the Word

Proverbs 6:1-5 (NIV)

> My son, if you have put up security for your neighbor, if you have struck hands in pledge for another, if you have been trapped by what you said, ensnared by the words of your mouth, then do this, my son, to free yourself, since you have fallen into your neighbor's hands: Go and humble yourself; press your plea with your neighbor! Allow no sleep to your eyes, no slumber to your eyelids. Free yourself, like a gazelle from the hand of the hunter, like a bird from the snare of the fowler.

Also read James 3:1-12.

Sometimes we need freedom from traps of our own making, especially when it comes to how we speak. In the case of the person spoken of in Proverbs, it was a matter of making rash promises to take the responsibility for someone else's debt. Solomon, in all his wisdom, advises against this practice and admonishes the one making the promise to "free himself" from his obligation.

How our words can entrap us! Verse two of the Proverbs passage says when you are "ensnared by the words of your mouth...**free yourself**."

Proverbs has much to say about the use of the tongue, and so does the New Testament. Much of the admonition found in the Epistles has to do with the use of the tongue. We can easily see that this is an area worthy of serious consideration!

Besides making rash promises, we are warned about speaking critically of others; taking God's name in vain; gossiping; angry outbursts; and fearful worrying, to name a few. We may even have to ask for forgiveness from those who we have offended. God says to us in this area of very human weakness: **free yourself**! Interestingly, God is not saying that He will free us, as if we have no control over what to say. We have to make a conscious decision to stop talking, confess our sins, and seek the forgiveness of the one who we have wronged. The passage in Proverbs gives three actions that are necessary in order to free ourselves:

1. Humble yourself—admit your mistake before God and before your neighbor.
2. Ask for forgiveness.
3. Be persistent.

All these actions require using words. In doing these three things, you will be using your tongue for good, and your humble words will set you free.

I have the kind of personality that shrinks from conflict of any kind. I am basically a peacemaker and I also want to please others. Sometimes these character traits are not admirable, for I find that trying to please other people all the time ties me up in knots. I am so afraid of confrontation that sometimes I don't even want to confront another person with truth (which they need to hear). In my desire to please others, I place myself in bondage to them and their opinions.

Free To Be

I recently had an experience that bears this out. In my job as a book editor, I occasionally have to turn down a request from an author who wants to use my services. This was the case with a particular author after I had already done two of her books. When she requested I do the third book, however, I just felt that I could not in good conscience continue. Reading through the second book brought many questions to my mind relating to the "rightness" of the teaching contained therein. I grew increasingly uneasy about encouraging this author to teach what I sensed was not very well supported by Scripture.

When it came time for me to tell her I had to decline from doing the third book, it took every bit of courage I had to follow through on what I believed was right. I hated to disappoint her and I did not want her to think badly of me. Nevertheless, God gave me the strength and the words to speak in communicating with her. God showed me that this was a step of faith for me—turning an author down at a time when I had no other work. He also showed me that I had gotten myself into this situation because I couldn't say, "No." I had accepted previous books even though I had reservations about the work in the beginning. Oh, how our words get us into trouble! This was a case when I had to "free myself" from my obligation, and it has been only through following God's leading in this matter that I now am free. I can feel good about doing what was right, even though at the time it was somewhat painful for me.

Questions to Ponder

Question 1: Can you think of an occasion when you spoke unwise words that have put you in someone else's debt?

Question 2: List the positive and negative uses of the tongue.

Memorize

James 1:19-20 (NIV)

"My dear brothers, take note of this: Everyone should be quick to listen, slow to speak and slow to become angry, for man's anger does not bring about the righteous life that God desires."

NOTES

Day 9

Freed from Sin – Slaves to Righteousness

From the Dictionary

Sin: Noun – Estrangement from God.

From the Word

Romans 7:23 (NIV)

> So I find this law at work: When I want to do good, evil is right there with me. For in my inner being I delight in God's law; but I see another law at work in the members of my body, waging war against the law of my mind and making me a prisoner of the law of sin at work within my members. What a wretched man I am! Who will rescue me from this body of death? Thanks be to God—through Jesus Christ our Lord!

Also read Romans 6; Romans 8:1-2.

It is difficult to grasp the fact than sin enslaves. When we are tempted to sin, the act of rebellion looks attractive. When we begin to focus on what sin has to offer in the way of pleasure, it becomes increasingly difficult to turn away from it. This is Satan's plotting—to appear as an "angel of light." (See 2 Corinthians 11:14.) Sin has great drawing power because it appeals to our natural instincts. We desire to have pleasure, power, and pride. No wonder it is so easy to become enslaved. Or, in the current vernacular—what a trip! Yielding to temptation requires no self-control, exercise of conscience, or sense of values. It is as if we are demanding two-year-olds. "I want" becomes the determining factor in what we choose to do. In reality, though, none of us want to get stuck in life as two-year-olds. We need and want to grow up, where we can make intelligent, responsible choices.

God knows, of course, our tendency to make the wrong choices when it comes to temptation. He knows we cannot live the righteous life on our own. He had to make a way for us to be righteous. Becoming a slave to righteousness by believing in Jesus Christ is the only way out of this "prison" of sin. Someone had to die to secure our freedom, and that Someone is Jesus. The only way out of the vicious cycle of sin and death is to reject our slavery to sin and embrace slavery to righteousness. So we go from "ever-increasing wickedness" (Romans 6:19) to "ever-increasing glory" (2 Corinthians 3:18), as we are transformed into His likeness.

Being a slave to sin has far-reaching consequences. So many times I have looked back at my life and regretted some of the choices I made that led to enslavement. At the time, I thought those choices would make me happy by experiencing pleasure. Those choices not only did not lead to happiness but also caused depression, feelings of guilt, and shame. The Apostle Paul experienced this same kind of struggle. He expressed his torment in Romans 7:23. Fortunately, for Paul and for us, in the very next verse he points to the One who can give us victory over the flesh—Jesus Christ. Then in Romans 8:1 (one of my favorites), Paul makes this powerful statement: "Therefore, there is now no condemnation for those who are in Christ Jesus." I have had to remind myself of this verse a multitude of times, for in this truth we are indeed free!

Questions to Ponder

Question 1: Can you think of a time in your life that you yielded to temptation, only to be caught in a trap of guilt and shame?

Question 2: Meditate on the sacrifice of Jesus for your sins and write down a prayer of gratitude.

Memorize

1 Corinthians 10:13

> "No temptation has seized you except what is common to man. And God is faithful; he will not let you be tempted beyond what you can bear. But when you are tempted, he will also provide a way out so that you can stand up under it."

NOTES

Day 10

Freedom from Death

From the Dictionary

"Death may be simply defined as the termination of life." (Easton's Illustrated Dictionary)

From the Word

John 3:16-18 (NIV)

> For God so loved the world that he gave his one and only Son, that whoever believes in him shall not perish but have eternal life. For God did not send his Son into the world to condemn the world, but to save the world through him. Whoever believes in him is not condemned, but whoever does not believe stands condemned already because he has not believed in the name of God's one and only Son.

Also read Romans 3:23; Hebrews 2; Revelation 3:20.

From the moment that Adam and Eve sinned in the Garden of Eden, mankind became subject to death—physical and spiritual death. Man would no longer be able to live in a perfect environment with nothing separating him from God's presence. Even today we live with the knowledge that we are ever dying.

What makes us fear death? Could it be just the fear of the unknown—not knowing about life after death? The natural man without Christ has much to fear, for even if he says he does not believe in God or an afterlife, the fact is he *will* face a righteous judgment. (Hebrews 9:27: "And as it is appointed unto men once to die, but after this the judgment.") I believe there is in man an innate knowledge of God. Regardless of how much one denies having this knowledge, he still has an innate fear that it is possible that God does exist and will hold him accountable for what he believes. We fear death because we fear judgment and punishment. The only thing that can calm our fears is professing Christ as the Son of God and receiving His mercy. Do you want to be free from the fear of judgment? Then heed the saving words of Jesus in John 3:16-18.

When I was a teenager I had a terrifying experience that caused me to freeze in panic. I remember that I was home alone that evening, and it was getting pretty late. I was talking on the phone with my friend Roy, having a nice conversation, when I noticed something unusual happening. Our phone was on a desk in the corner between the kitchen and living room, and I had a clear view of the back door. As I stood there talking, I was facing the door, and I began to see the doorknob moving. The door was locked, and I didn't expect my parents back from their outing yet, so it became apparent that someone was trying to break in. My heart started to beat rapidly and my mind began to race as I considered a possible course of action. I have never thought of myself as being particularly courageous, and I certainly didn't like confrontation either, so my thoughts were primarily those of, "How do I get out of here?!" Since I had Roy on the phone, I lowered my voice and told him what was happening. His response was to tell me to stay put and he would be there in just a few minutes to rescue me. Now he only lived three blocks away, so I thought he could make it over to my house before something dire happened to me. Though I was reluctant to break off communication with him by hanging up, I knew he could not be with me in person until I did hang up. (That was long before the advent of the ever-present ear accessory called a cell phone.)

I remember hanging up the phone and going to sit on the couch that was close to the front door. That way I didn't have to continue to watch the jiggling doorknob. I sat down and waited, paralyzed with panic. If someone did break in, I'm not sure I could have moved!

My imagination took over, and I began to wonder what sort of person (probably a man) would be trying to get into our house. We lived right behind a shopping center and there was a dark alley running alongside our fence line. There had been a number of times when boys had climbed over the fence and cut across our backyard as a shortcut to get to our street. My mind worked overtime, imagining some of those boys coming from the alley to try to break into our house.

It didn't take Roy long to get to my house. He ran all the way and made it in about five minutes. For me, though, it was the longest five minutes of my life! I felt paralyzed with fear and suspended in time. It was even difficult for me to go to the front door when Roy knocked. My rescuer was there—I could be safe—but I had to go open the door and let him in. My fears were relieved when Roy investigated and found that the intruder had gone, and I breathed a sigh of relief just knowing that I no longer had to face the situation alone.

In a way, life is like the frightening occurrence that I had experienced. Before we come to Christ, we are in the dark concerning God's existence and the afterlife. We go through life worried about the future, desperately trying to find a savior to deliver us from the evils of this world. Evil is there at the back door of our lives, trying to break in and capture our very souls. That is the bad news. The good news is that we have a Savior who has been sent to rescue us from sin and death. Our deliverance is at hand—we just have to open the door of our hearts and allow Jesus, the Deliverer, to come in. When we are secure in Him, we no longer have to fear death but can welcome it because we have the promise of eternal life with Him in Heaven.

Ephesians 1:7-10 (Message)

> Because of the sacrifice of the Messiah, his blood poured out on the altar of the Cross, we're a free people— free of penalties and punishments chalked up by all our misdeeds. And not just barely free, either. *Abundantly* free! He thought of everything, provided for everything we could possibly need, letting us in on the plans he took such delight in making. He set it all out before us in Christ, a long-range plan in which everything would be brought together and summed up in him, everything in deepest heaven, everything on planet earth.

Questions to Ponder

Question 1: What is it about death that you fear?

Question 2: Have you secured your deliverance from eternal death?

Memorize

Hebrews 2:14-15 (NIV)

> "Since the children have flesh and blood, he too shared in their humanity so that by his death he might destroy him who holds the power of death—that is, the devil—and free those who all their lives were held in slavery by their fear of death."

Free To Be

<u>NOTES</u>

Day 11

Free from Darkness

From the Dictionary

Free: Adjective - Not fixed in position.

From the Word

John 13:30 (NIV)

> "As soon as Judas had taken the bread, he went out. And it was night."

Also read John 12:46; John 13:30; Isaiah 9:1-2; Matthew 4:16; John 1:4-5.

John 13:30 tells us of Judas as he prepared to betray Jesus. Take note that as he went out (to carry out his plan), "it was night." The night had fallen on Judas' soul as well, as is true for every person who rejects Jesus Christ as Messiah. Shortly after Judas betrayed Jesus, the soldiers came and took Jesus to the trial that would lead Him to the cross. It was still night. It began to look like the forces of darkness were winning, for Jesus Himself was THE LIGHT who had come into the world. As that night passed, with all its illegalities and irregularities, it became more and more apparent that the darkness (sinfulness of man) would defeat the Son of God.

Even as He hung on the cross at mid-day, darkness overtook the land for several hours. As Jesus bore our sins on that cruel cross, He Himself entered the world of darkness. Oh, but praise God, though there seemed to be no escaping from the darkness, Jesus convincingly showed that He was THE LIGHT by rising from the dead after three days. The Light has shown again in the lives of Christians through the ages and is still available today to bring us out of darkness, if we will place our trust in Him.

We who believe in Jesus Christ walk in the light. The light penetrates the dark places of our souls that are overcome with sin. We not only have the light, but as Jesus said to His followers, we *are* the light (Matthew 5:14). It is the person who rejects Jesus, just as Judas did, who lives in darkness. How can we be free from the darkness? Our only hope that the sun will rise in our souls and last through eternity comes because we trust in the Light, Jesus Christ.

A person who is in the Light will:
1. Be enlightened – know the truth.
2. Be able to see the road before him.
3. Show the way to others.
4. Be able to dispel the darkness through confession and repentance of sin.

We learn to walk in the light more and more as we read God's Word, pray, and fellowship with other Christians. We also have an obligation to share that light with others who are still groping in the dark.

When I was a girl, I remember going to camp for several summers. I had to pack the usual gear needed for lots of outdoor activities. Some of these activities were at night. It was a pretty rustic camp setting, and the restroom facility was in a separate building from our cabins. Of necessity, we had to have flashlights on hand so that we could maneuver through the campground in the dark. A flashlight is a wonderful tool to have when one needs to move forward in the dark. It's kind of scary to go into unfamiliar territory

Free To Be

when everything is draped in darkness. A flashlight, though, only allows you to see what is ahead just a few feet in front of you. This is like the Word of God at times. His light (Scripture) gives us a view of the path just ahead. Though we cannot see far into the future and we do not know what awaits us "out there," we learn to trust God to provide the enlightenment that we need when the time comes. Escape from darkness comes in our relationship with God. As long as we stay on His paths, trusting Him, we will walk in the light and have His promise that He will never leave us nor forsake us.

Questions to Ponder

Question 1: Are there dark places in your soul?

Question 2: List the qualities of light and how it helps us.

Question 3: Compare the qualities of light with what spiritual light does.

Memorize

Psalms 119:105 (NIV)

> **"Your word is a lamp to my feet and a light for my path."**

NOTES

Day 12

Free from Blindness

From the Dictionary

Blindness: Noun – lack of sight.

From the Word
John 9:1-4

> Now as *Jesus* passed by, He saw a man who was blind from birth. And His disciples asked Him, saying, "Rabbi, who sinned, this man or his parents, that he was born blind?" Jesus answered, "Neither this man nor his parents sinned, but that the works of God should be revealed in him. I must work the works of Him who sent Me while it is day; *the* night is coming when no one can work.

Also read all of chapter of John 9.

In the scriptures we see Jesus encountering the blindness of the Pharisees, which was a deep spiritual blindness. The encounter with the Pharisees occurred after a miracle of healing took place. Jesus and his disciples were going along their way and happened to pass a blind man. The disciples, steeped in their preconceptions about suffering and punishment, asked Jesus, "Rabbi, who sinned, this man or his parents, that he was born blind?" (John 9:2 NIV). It would seem that the disciples were more interested in a theological discussion than they were concerned for the blind man.

Jesus, however, cared and he healed the man, who was subsequently brought before the Pharisees and subjected to much questioning. The man did not know all the ramifications of his healing, but he knew that once he was blind but now he could see. Jesus used this encounter as a teaching opportunity to show that the spiritual blindness of the Pharisees was far worse than the beggar's physical blindness, for the beggar confessed his faith in Jesus as Messiah, while the Pharisees did not.

What can we learn from this incident in the life of Jesus? We must evaluate our own visual capability. Are we too spiritually blind? I have a friend who became physically blind several years ago and I have asked her to be a guest writer for this day's lesson. Here is her story in the form of a drama:

The heavy, black velvet curtain descended slowly at the close of Act II. A hush descended upon the audience. At the conclusion of this second act, one patron was heard to murmur, "That last scene took an unexpected, tragic turn."

Synopsis of Acts I and II

The protagonist, Joann, had accepted Jesus Christ as her Savior at age seven. She had been reared in a loving, supportive home by Christian parents. Joann attended a Christian college on an academic scholarship and served as president of her denomination's student union during her senior year. After teaching three years and attending graduate school, she returned to find that the most intelligent, most handsome, finest Christian boy in her high school had also turned into the most eligible bachelor in her hometown. Within two weeks, she and Roy were engaged; within three months, they were married. He was the only man she had ever dated who was as committed as she to giving God His tithe and their offerings. They were blessed with a handsome brunette son and a beautiful blonde daughter, whom they named Rex and Ronda. These twins were healthy, intelligent, and a total joy. Both Joann's parents and Roy's parents lived to celebrate their sixty-plus wedding anniversaries. Joann was successful in her chosen career as an English teacher. She taught students from seventh graders through sophomores in college.

Toward the end of the second act, she remarked, "I love teaching; during the day I teach at the high school, in the evenings I teach at the college, and on Sundays Roy and I teach a Sunday School class for young singles." It was in the midst of this busy but fulfilling schedule that Joann was diagnosed with a meningioma tumor surrounding her pituitary gland and both optic nerves. Surgery to remove this tumor left Joann blind; thus, the black curtain fell.

The intermission between Acts II and III was lengthy enough for many to speculate on the coming drama.

This time, the black curtain did not ascend to signify the opening of the final act. An audience member whispered to another, "This may be a unique experience. Have you ever been to a play performed without lights?"

"No, but God will intervene; the lights will come on. You'll see."

But the darkness remained. Joann experienced utter desolation, both within her soul and within her surroundings. She struggled to find a purpose for her life and a reason to live. Upon realizing that her livelihood and her independence had been taken from her, she even felt that death would be preferable to blindness. The audience watched, unable to rectify her situation and bring light into her life again. People who knew The Light began to petition God on Joann's behalf. Others were only able to watch helplessly as Joann coped with her darkness.

Through much soul searching, Joann realized that her new occupation would be intercessory prayer. Instead of thinking about herself so much, she would concentrate on the needs and struggles of others. With each day, her situation grew lighter. This light was reflected from her husband and children, her Sunday School class members, and her church friends.

Lightness permeates her days while she shares the prayer requests of others. Eventually, she even gave thanks to God for removing many of the distractions in her day to day life, allowing her to focus on her prayers while talking with her Heavenly Father. She experienced this truth as she remembered the words from a song she had sung all her life: "the things of earth grow strangely dim in the light of his glory and grace" ("Turn Your Eyes Upon Jesus," Copyright 1922 Singspiration Music).

She realized that God had called her to serve as a witness and to remind each of us that we will come before Jesus at the seat of Judgment. Some will stand before the Son of God and He will say, "Depart from me; I never knew you." They will be cast into outer darkness." She hastens to add, "I am now experiencing darkness, but it is only a *temporary* darkness." The darkness caused by the permanent separation from God is a situation she would wish upon no one. She states that she would not be able to stand this blindness that she is in now in were it not for the grace that God gives her every day.

Jesus said, "Not everyone who says 'Lord, Lord!' will enter into the kingdom of Heaven, but he who does the will of my father who sent me." Although her life is not what she expected it to be in Act III, she strives each day to know and follow God's will.

Her first grandchild, Caleb Brock Murray, was born in December. Though she has not yet seen his face, she has faith that for all eternity they will enjoy fellowship. God's strength endures to all generations.

Joann Northen, Belton, Texas

Today, Joann is an inspiration to all who know her. We rarely see her engaged in self-pity. She is almost always smiling, and she cares for others with God's unconditional love. However, the thing about her that impresses us the most is her great spiritual insights. God has not chosen to renew her physical sight at this time, but He has blessed her and blesses others through her as she "sees" things that many of us miss. Oh, that we all would have our spiritual eyes opened, that we might walk in the Light of the Lord, for this is God's purpose for each of us. In predicting the coming of the Messiah and His work, Isaiah says of Him:

> I will lead the blind by ways they have not known, along unfamiliar paths I will guide them; I will turn the darkness into light before them and make the rough places smooth.
>
> These are the things I will do; I will not forsake them. Isaiah 42:16 (NIV)

Questions to Ponder

Question 1: Have you ever had your spiritual eyes opened,

giving you insight into a particular matter?

Question 2: In times of suffering, do you look to God for His purposes to be worked out in your life?

Memorize

1 John 1:5-7

> **God is light; in Him there is no darkness at all. If we claim to have fellowship with Him yet walk in the darkness, we lie and do not live the truth. But if we walk in the light, as He is in the light, we have fellowship with one another, and the blood of Jesus, His Son, purifies us from all sin.**

NOTES

Day 13

Free from Bondage to the Past

From the Dictionary

Confinement: Noun – The act of restraining of a person's liberty by confining [him].

From the Word

Hebrews 12:1 (NIV)

> Therefore, since we are surrounded by such a great cloud of witnesses, let us throw off everything that hinders and the sin that so easily entangles, and let us run with perseverance the race marked out for us.

Also read John 11.

John 11 tells us the story of the resurrection of Jesus' friend Lazarus. This miracle was pivotal in leading to Jesus' arrest, trial, and crucifixion. The Jewish religious leaders, rather than focusing on the resurrected life of Lazarus, could only think of how they could put Jesus to death. They preferred the bondage of their earthbound thinking (much like the grave clothes that were wrapped around Lazarus's dead body) over being willing to risk their positions in society. They clung to their fears, and those fears choked the life out of them, keeping them from the eternal life that comes to those who believe in Jesus.

Though the religious leaders were bound, real freedom

from bondage came to those who believed Jesus when He said He was the Resurrection and the Life. Only as the sisters expressed their belief that Jesus was who He said He was did they begin to be relieved in grieving over the loss of their brother. It was a process of belief that led to relief. We can see this same process in our lives as we allow God to deliver us from bondage. The process I see taking place is as follows:

1. A relationship is established – "the one you love is sick" (John 11:3). Lazarus and his sisters had become close friends of Jesus and supporters of His ministry. Jesus had taken the time to develop a relationship with them in order to bless them. Our relationships with others are often the channel through which God blesses us. Beyond our relationship with Jesus, it is also important to establish loving relationships with other believers so that when the time comes for our "release" from bondage, we can have supporters and prayer warriors ready to come alongside.

2. Jesus is aware of the need – "So the sisters sent word to Jesus…" (John 11:3). Jesus saw the needs of His friends, and He sees and knows our needs as well. He knows what has happened to us and the burdens we carry. He knows even before we acknowledge them.

3. Jesus responds to our needs in His time – "Yet when he heard that Lazarus was sick, he stayed where he was two more days" (John 11:6). We need to have faith in God's timing while we suffer from being in bondage. Even after Jesus was told of Lazarus's sickness, He delayed going to him. He was not calloused toward the suffering of his dearly loved friends. He was just sensitive to God's timing, knowing that when God sent Him to intervene, the Lord would be glorified.

Not only would God be glorified, but the miracle of resurrection would also be far greater than a miracle of healing would have been.

In my own journey of healing, I believe God revealed to me my bondage only when I was able to deal with it (in my case, early adulthood). It takes patience and faith to believe that God will do a work of deliverance from our bondage to the past. Oh, but when the time came for me to be loosed from my bondage, I could fully realize God's miracle of healing!

4. Jesus had authority over death – "Jesus said to her, 'I am the resurrection and the life. He who believes in me will live, even though he dies; and whoever lives and believes in me will never die. Do you believe this?'" (John 11:25-26). When Jesus spoke the words, "Lazarus, come out!" the chains of death were broken. The chains of death are broken for us who believe in Jesus as our Savior and Lord. We are delivered from the final eternal death, but we are also delivered from the dying that takes place in us when we choose to remain in our chains of bitterness, fear, and anger.

5. The purposes of God supersede our individual needs – "Therefore many of the Jews who had come to visit Mary, and had seen what Jesus did, put their faith in him" (John 11:45). Although it is difficult to understand why we go through certain trials and experience different kinds of bondage, we can through faith see through God's eyes. Many times this kind of vision does not come except in retrospect.

6. Grave wrappings – Jesus said to them, "Take off the grave clothes and let him go" (John 11:44 NIV). The grave wrappings, or clothes, were like bandages wrapped around the body, with a separate cloth to cover the face. First, Jesus had

commanded that the stone be rolled away (after He had comforted Mary and Martha), giving an escape route for the risen Lazarus. I believe that each of the bandages represent things that have caused me to be bound—things like fear, insecurity, a sense of abandonment, an extreme need to please others, anger, and depression. Though I had been victimized as a child, I did not realize how bound by fear I was until early adulthood. I had already established a loving relationship with Jesus, and one by one these "grave clothes" have been removed from me. Now I am free to serve God fully, trusting that He can use me to point others to Jesus, the "Resurrection and the Life."

Questions to Ponder

Question 1: Are there things in your past that have you bound by fear, anger, or bitterness? Pray and ask God to reveal to you what is holding you back from being all God wants you to be.

Question 2: Is there someone you know to whom God is calling you to minister healing words of encouragement and hope? Open your eyes to God's work in those around you.

Memorize

Hebrews 12:1 (NIV)

"Therefore, since we are surrounded by such a great cloud of witnesses, let us throw off everything that hinders and the sin that so easily entangles, and let us run with perseverance the race marked out for us."

NOTES

Day 14

Freedom from Thirst

From the Dictionary

Thirst: Verb – Have a craving, appetite, or great desire for.

From the Word

Matthew 5:6 (NIV)

> "Blessed are those who hunger and thirst for righteousness, for they will be filled."

Also read John 4.

In John 4 we are told the story of Jesus' encounter with the woman of Sychar, Samaria, which according to long-held tradition was the location for "Jacob's well." This part of Israel is a very dry area, and the importance of the city well cannot be understated. Jacob's well certainly was a treasure and a source of life-giving water in the physical realm. The well, established long before, gave silent witness to the coming Messiah, who would bring "living water" that, when partaken of, would lead to eternal life.

In visiting Israel in 1996, I was impressed with how much of the Promised Land is actually desert and wilderness. Water is a very precious commodity. Much of Israel's history has to do with water—from crossing the Red Sea and later the Jordan, to entering the Promised Land, to the building of Hezekiah's tunnel in Jerusalem in order to get water to that city built on a rock. Many of Jesus' teachings had to do with water and thirst. He even called Himself "the Living Water." How much this must have meant to the people living in desert conditions! It required a lot of hard work to bring water into the household for daily needs.

The woman who came to the well of Jacob may have thought of her encounter with the unusual Jewish man like this:

> I'm here to tell you about love—real love. I used to think I knew what love was, like so many people do. For a lot of people, "love" means having a physical relationship. And believe me, I know all about that. You see, I've had five husbands and have "known" more men than that. Yes, I thought I knew about love...but one day I found out there was something more than what I had experienced.
>
> In my village in Samaria, it is the custom of the women to go and draw water at the well outside the city, usually in the cool of the morning or evening. But it was different for me. I knew that if I went when the other women did, I would be scorned. My reputation wasn't too good, and well...frankly, I didn't like being reminded of my guilty lifestyle by hearing the whispers and enduring the looks of condemnation. So, I went to the well alone, at noonday. It was hot, unbearably so, but the heat was easier to bear than the women's stares and gossip.
>
> It was on such a day that something very special happened to me. When I got to the well, there was a man there—a Jewish man. I was shocked when He actually spoke to me—me, a woman and a Samaritan! Most Jews were very prejudiced against us, so at best I thought I would be ignored by this man. Now, I was used to having men speak to me

(usually only men spoke to me), but the kinds of things they said were very different from the words spoken to me this day.

This man started by asking me for a drink of water—to draw Him one from the well. Then He proceeded to tell me about a living water that I could have, where I would never thirst again. Well, He certainly had my attention! It would have been nice not to have to come to the well every day. But I was soon to find out that He was not speaking of water to meet my physical needs. This man (whom I found out later was called Jesus) saw in me a great thirst—a spiritual thirst. He astounded me by telling me the truth not only about myself but the truth about God. This was living water indeed! He wasn't even deterred when I tried to divert His attention with a religious argument. Instead, He was patient with me, gently guiding me back to my need.

Yes, this Jesus knew my thirst—a thirst that had not been quenched by anything or anyone else. That thirst was to know love—to be loved and accepted by God, and to know forgiveness. And here was someone offering me that very thing. And I accepted the offer by believing that this Jesus was my Messiah. It was the best news I'd ever heard, and I had to run and tell everyone in town. It no longer mattered what others thought of me. I was changed—a new person, and I wanted others to know how they too could be changed. I know there are many who, like me, are thirsting for real love and their needs can only be met by the living water that Jesus the Messiah can give. ("Samaritan Woman" monologue by Kay Coulter, unpublished)

Physical water was necessary to grow crops. The result

of the woman's partaking of the Living Water was that there was a great spiritual harvest of souls in Sychar as the people also believed in the Christ.

Questions to Ponder

Question 1: Do the things that you pursue satisfy your spiritual thirst?

Question 2: Make a plan to study God's Word on a regular basis, and keep a journal to record ways that Scripture quenches your thirst.

Question 3: Do you know others who are thirsting for love? Will you tell them about the Living Water?

Memorize

John 4:13-14 (NIV)

> **"Jesus answered, 'Everyone who drinks this water will be thirsty again, but whoever drinks the water I give him will never thirst. Indeed, the water I give him will become in him a spring of water welling up to eternal life.'"**

NOTES

Day 15

Liberty Is Not License

From the Dictionary

License – Noun: Freedom to deviate deliberately from normally applicable rules or practices (especially in behavior or speech).

From the Word

Galatians 5:13 (KJV)

> For, brethren, ye have been called unto liberty; only *use* not liberty for an occasion to the flesh, but by love serve one another.

Also read 1 Peter 2:16; 2 Corinthians 3:17-18; Romans 12:1-2.

In the early church, there was quite a problem with Christians coming from very pagan backgrounds. In Paul's and Peter's letters to these early Christians, each addressed this matter of freedom in Christ. The book of Galatians was written to address the problems of a church of extremes: those who insisted on legalism and those who thought God's grace was a license to do anything they pleased. Some thought and taught that if we are saved through Christ, our eternal destiny is secure, so it really did not matter what we did here on earth because the physical body had no spiritual value. How like the American Church today! When are we going to learn that what we do with our bodies does count? Christians are called upon to live responsibly in a world that is irresponsible. How else can we stand out? How else can we attract others to Jesus?

I remember when I was in high school; my English teacher required our class to write an essay about freedom with responsibility. The intent of the assignment was to make us think about the responsibilities that come with democracy. This assignment really caused me to think. Americans are so proud of our freedoms, yet we have allowed our country to function with freedom without responsibility. Our freedoms are greatly eroded when we allow an "anything goes" attitude. After all, we have to be tolerant (or at least speak with all political correctness)! Yes, we as a nation are tolerant—of all kinds of foolish behavior. Has this made us stronger? No. There seems to be a demand for "rights" that was never intended by the writers of our Constitution. Freedom without responsibility takes us down the slippery slope from democracy to anarchy.

In the spiritual realm, we need to heed the cautions in Scripture about misusing our freedoms. Paul spent a great deal of time correcting the error of thinking in both the legalists and the "free spirits," those who thought they were free to sin without consequences. He follows his admonition to "not use your freedom to indulge the sinful nature," with a contrasting command—that of **serving one another in love**.

Peter addressed this issue in his first epistle to the Christian Jews who were scattered abroad, living in many different cultures and under pagan governments. He gives them the same exhortation, "Live as free men, but do not use your freedom as a cover-up for evil; live as **servants** of God."

So, from Paul we are exhorted to **love** and from Peter we are exhorted to **serve**. True freedom (with responsibility) is summed up in 2 Corinthians 3:17 (NIV): "Now the Lord is the Spirit, and where the Spirit of the Lord is, there is freedom."

Questions to Ponder

Question 1: Is there some way that you are using your freedom in Christ to indulge in ungodly living?

Question 2: List some responsibilities that come with freedom under grace.

Memorize

2 Corinthians 3:17

> **"Now the Lord is the Spirit, and where the Spirit of the Lord is, there is freedom."**

NOTES

Day 16

Substitute or Satisfaction

From the Dictionary

Satisfaction: Noun – State of being gratified.

From the Word

Luke 4:4 (KJV)

"It is written, That man shall not live by bread alone, but by every word of God."

Also read Luke 4:1-13.

When Jesus was being tempted by Satan in the wilderness, He answered Satan's attempts to draw Him away from God's purpose by quoting Scripture. In this case, Satan appealed to Jesus' physical appetite, tempting Him to turn the stones into bread. Jesus replied with the quote from Deuteronomy 8:3. Jesus also taught the disciples this same principle when He answered them concerning His needs as He was ministering the words of life to the Samaritan woman (John 4:5). Jesus was tempted to accept substitutes in place of true satisfaction in God, but He did not yield to temptation and therefore remained sinless.

Our society is so focused on satisfying our fleshly appetites. Just look at the ads for "all you can eat" buffets; supersized meals at fast food restaurants; indulgence in sweets (after all, you're worth it!); etc. The irony is that while we have gone after these substitutes, eating and drinking excessively, we have become a nation with an extreme obesity problem and are always seeking new ways to lose weight. Yes, we want to "have our cake and eat it, too," regardless of the consequences.

This not only applies to our eating more and more, but also in our other fleshly appetites: sex, status, power, popularity, wealth, etc. We have all these things available to us, and there is a sense that because we live in a "free" democratic society, it is our "right" to be successful in our pursuit of happiness.

It is true that we have the constitutional right to the pursuit of happiness, but what many fail to see is that these pursuits of worldly things do not bring happiness.

Jesus taught that doing the will of God is what brings satisfaction and joy (Matthew 6:33), and that God will meet all our needs (Hebrews 11:6). We need to appropriate God's freedom in our lives by looking to Him for satisfaction, for He has promised that He will meet our needs. If we trust Him to provide, then we are free to give ourselves away, investing in others' lives, that they too may know the satisfaction of having their sins forgiven and experiencing the glories of a relationship with God.

Questions to Ponder

Question 1: What are some substitutes that you may be accepting in place of the satisfaction that comes from doing God's will?

Question 2: How does pursuing the things of God bring you satisfaction?

Memorize

Hebrews 11:6 (NIV)

"And without faith it is impossible to please God, because anyone who comes to him must believe that he exists and that he rewards those who earnestly seek him."

NOTES

Day 17

Free to Worship

From the Dictionary

Worship: Noun – A feeling of profound love and admiration.

From the Word

Luke 10:41-42 (NIV):

"Martha, Martha," the Lord answered, "you are worried and upset about many things, but only one thing is needed. Mary has chosen what is better, and it will not be taken away from her."

Also read Luke 10:38-42; Luke 8:11-15; Matthew 6:27.

That elusive thing we call "time" often controls our lives and *T – I – M – E* is ticking away. We arise in the mornings with alarm clocks announcing the urgency of getting out of bed. This sets the stage for the whole day. We are pressed to be ready on time, to arrive wherever on time, to rush to the next appointment, to pick up kids, to prepare meals, to go to work, to go to church, etc., etc., etc.

The minute hand on the clock drives us as if each minute of time has to be filled with activity. This attention to the clock's ticking minutes away indicates our anxiety over the demands of the world around us. We get so caught up in "doing" that we neglect "being." Jesus spoke to this very common human tendency when He told the parable of the sower and the seed (Luke 8:11-15). You may recall that some of the seed fell on thorny ground. In interpreting His parable, Jesus said that the thorny ground represented those whose lives are choked by worries, riches, and pleasures. Do these three things not sum up our pursuits? Pursuing riches may just mean we are making a living, striving to provide for our families. Pursuing pleasures has to do with how we use our leisure time. And worries? Well, worries are...worries! How much time do we spend worrying about things that will never happen? The "what ifs" of life can dominate our thinking. Jesus said in another passage, "Who of you by worrying can add a single hour to his life?" (Matthew 6:27). I say that not only will worrying not add to your life, but it also will actually take away from the quality of your life.

How can we be free from the cares of this world and turn our attention to worshipping the Lord? Throughout the Bible, God seems to be more interested in our "being" than in our "doing." We need to evaluate our relationship with the Father. What does He want us to **be**?

In the Luke passage that relates the story of Martha and Mary, what God wants us to **be** is very evident. To illustrate each of their mindsets, an equation might look like this:

$$\text{Martha} = \text{Worry}$$
$$\text{Mary} = \text{Worship}$$

Which one had it right? Mary, of course. Jesus clearly states that Mary had chosen the better way. How can we develop a Mary mindset—one that emphasizes worship (being in God's presence) rather than worry (caught up in the cares of this world)? We must **choose** the better way. This does not mean neglecting necessary activities (making a living, taking care of family, etc.); it just means that we choose to free ourselves from the tyranny of the urgent. We can plan our days around worship time. Make it a priority.

Have an attitude of prayer, connecting with the Father throughout the day. Read, study, meditate on, and memorize Scripture. For instance, as we become very familiar with passages like the one in Matthew that reminds us that when we get caught up in life's pressures we should not worry but rather trust God to meet our needs, we can take a moment, take a breath, and calm down. Breathe in the truth of God's Word on a regular basis and you will find yourself becoming free from the cares of this world.

Questions to Ponder

Question 1: Do you see yourself more as a Martha or a Mary?

Question 2: Do you let the clock rule your life?

Question 3: What are some things you can do to change your worry into worship? List these and decide to change.

Memorize

Mark 12:30 (KJV)

"Love the Lord your God with all your heart and with all your soul and with all your mind and with all your strength."

NOTES

Day 18

Free from Prejudice

From the Dictionary

Prejudice: Noun - A partiality that prevents objective consideration of an issue or situation.

From the Word

Acts 10:34-35 (NIV)

> Then Peter began to speak: "I now realize how true it is that God does not show favoritism but accepts men from every nation who fear him and do what is right."

Also read Luke 7:1-10.

In this passage we learn of Jesus' healing of the centurion's servant. A Roman centurion was a soldier in charge of a hundred men. It is interesting to note how the centurions were viewed in the first century Jewish culture.

> The centurions mentioned in the New Testament are uniformly spoken of in terms of praise, whether in the Gospels or in the Acts. It is interesting to compare this with the statement of Polybius (vi. 24), that the centurions were chosen by merit, and so were men remarkable not so much for their daring courage as for their deliberation, constancy, and strength of mind (Dr. Maclear's N. T. History—

Easton's Illustrated Dictionary).

The centurion who sent word to Jesus to heal his servant must have been courageous. He was not a Jew, nor would he have been looking for a Messiah. Somehow he had come to believe that Jesus had miraculous powers and that God was "no respecter of persons" (KJV). The fact that Jesus did not turn him away is evidence of his equality. Jesus' healings always taught people about the kind of God we serve. He is a God of compassion and He shows no favoritism. His grace is free to all who believe, regardless of race, gender, or station in life. In this passage, Jesus healed the centurion's servant and pointed out that this Gentile's faith was greater than any He had seen in Israel (verse 9). His words must have been shocking to the Jews, though they did admit their admiration for this particular Gentile (verse 4).

Other incidents that show God's love, grace, and impartiality are Jesus' encounter with the Samaritan woman at Sychar; Paul's call to preach to the Gentiles; and Peter's dream in Acts 10. We also learn from the genealogy of Jesus that there were Gentiles in His ancestry—Rahab and Ruth. We can learn from these passages that in order to live obediently in God's Kingdom, we must see the world through His eyes—without prejudice toward anyone.

God taught me well how to overcome prejudice in my life. The family in which I was brought up taught me to hate, fear, and feel superior to people of other races—particularly blacks and Mexicans (at that time they were not called African-Americans and Hispanics). Since I graduated from high school before integration really took hold, I was not around very many people "of color." When I married, I carried into my adulthood all those negative messages about other races. Knowing that I needed to change my mindset about this issue, God gave me opportunity to minister to others different than I am.

Free To Be

One of these opportunities came when I was a young married woman. Our church sent sixty volunteers to the Texas/Mexico border to conduct Vacation Bible Schools. Of course, this meant I would be working with Mexican children. During that week, I learned two important lessons: (1) No matter the race, we all need Jesus and the salvation He offers; and (2) Sometimes we are called upon to witness and minister to people whom we will never see again. This meant trusting God to cultivate the seeds we had planted, never seeing the lasting fruit of our efforts.

Since that time, God has given me a love for other races and cultures and a desire to minister to them. I came to love the little children I worked with that week in Nuevo Laredo, and even the language barrier (I had 4-year-olds who didn't speak English) did not keep the love of Jesus from shining through. I remember making a conscious choice to overcome my prejudice, and when I did, I became open to receive many blessings. How enriched my life has been in accepting others without prejudice! It is wonderful to know I am free from the stereotypes and preconceived ideas of my generation.

Questions to Ponder

Question 1: In examining your heart, do you know of some prejudice that you have against others?

Question 2: As you pray, allow God to reveal to you the preconceived ideas which need to be changed.

Memorize

John 3:16-18 (NIV)

[16] For God so loved the world that he gave his one and only Son, that whoever believes in him shall

not perish but have eternal life. [17] For God did not send his Son into the world to condemn the world, but to save the world through him. [18] Whoever believes in him is not condemned, but whoever does not believe stands condemned already because he has not believed in the name of God's one and only Son.

NOTES

Day 19

Free from Greed

From the Dictionary

To free: Verb - Part with a possession or right.

From the Word
Luke 12:15 (NIV)

> "Then he [Jesus] said to them, 'Watch out! Be on your guard against all kinds of greed; a man's life does not consist in the abundance of his possessions.'"

Also read Luke 12:13-21; Matthew 6:20-21; Colossians 3:5

Greed is motivated by selfishness and self-centeredness. I also believe that fear is a factor in greed, at least for some. I can be fearful that my needs will not be provided for, so I grasp and cling to my money and possessions as if there were no tomorrow. A person who is greedy is focused only on himself and often is blind to the needs of others. Greed shows lack of trust in God, for a greedy person does not believe God will provide for him. There is never an "enough" measure for the greedy person—no real satisfaction. Note that the farmer in the parable had to tell himself to "eat, drink, and be merry." This was not genuine joy and satisfaction but rather a forced and faked happiness. Jesus didn't say we should not have material blessings or that being rich is a bad thing. He just said our focus needs to be on being "rich toward God" (Luke 12:21).

I remember a Christmas musical that my church choir did a few years ago. It was a contemporized version of the Christmas story, with the songs having lyrics that were very pertinent in our society today. One of the songs was a solo by the innkeeper who had no room for Mary and Joseph. In the setting of the play, this character was portrayed as a very greedy man, who only wanted paying customers and had little compassion for the needy. When asked by his wife and friends how much money it would take to satisfy him, he replied, "Just a little bit more." This number was done humorously, but the lesson is clear. One who is greedy and who only thinks of himself will never know what "enough" is.

In recent days, as well as other times in my life, God has shown me that I was spending too much money on clothes. I like pretty clothes, I like to dress fashionably, and I enjoy creating outfits. Now, I know there is nothing inherently evil about having pretty clothes. God knows we need to be clothed! However, it is possible to become greedy and self-indulgent in this area. I already have more than I need, so I believe God is leading me to be a better steward of my finances. In praying on this issue, I have come to the conclusion that God wants me to direct these funds I might have spent on clothes beyond my needs into His Kingdom's work. With this conviction came an immediate opportunity. I have a friend who is working for a non-profit ministry that helps the hungry and evangelizes the lost. She has to raise her own support and she is the sole breadwinner right now in her family. God impressed upon me to contribute monthly to her support. How rewarding it is for me as I listen to my friend's stories of how she is able to lead people to Christ through her ministry! Knowing I have contributed to this effort reminds me of Matthew 6:20-21 (KJV): "But lay up for yourselves treasures in heaven, where neither moth nor rust doth corrupt, and where thieves do not break through nor steal: For where your treasure is, there will your heart be also." God has freed me from greed, I have been able to help someone else, and I don't even miss having more clothes to crowd into my closets.

Questions to Ponder

Question 1: As you read the Scripture passage for this lesson, did God bring to mind an area of your life in which you are greedy?

Question 2: Are your eyes open to the needs of others?

Question 3: What are some specific things you can do to develop an outward focus that leads you to help others?

Memorize

Matthew 19:21 (NIV)

"Jesus answered, 'If you want to be perfect, go, sell your possessions and give to the poor, and you will have treasure in heaven. Then come, follow me.'"

NOTES

Day 20

Free from Condemnation

From the Dictionary

Condemnation: Noun - The condition of being strongly disapproved of.

From the Word

Romans 8:1-2

> There is therefore now no condemnation to them which are in Christ Jesus, who walk not after the flesh, but after the Spirit. For the law of the Spirit of life in Christ Jesus hath made me free from the law of sin and death.

Also read John 8:1-11; John 3:16-18; Romans 6:23; Revelation 22:17

God has provided a way for us to no longer be condemned, though we are all guilty of sin. As humans, we carry the cloak of condemnation because of our own sinfulness. In our society there are those who try to deny that there are such things as sin and guilt. Yet the psychiatrists' offices are full of patients who do not know what to do about the guilt within them. No amount of denial or assurances from a counselor that there is no need to feel guilty will bring peace of mind.

There is a false guilt from which many victims suffer. In a *"USA Today"* poll taken in August of 1995, "34 percent of people polled" said they felt "guilty for nothing in particular." This is the kind of guilt that keeps a person living in fear—that is, the fear that he might have inadvertently sinned and might need to be punished, even if he has to punish himself.

There is also a true guilt, and it needs to be dealt with appropriately. We are allowed to feel true guilt in order for God to capture our attention and lead us to repentance. God knew that we could not atone for our own guilt, so He provided a way of salvation devoid of human effort. In order to be free of guilt someone has to pay for our sins. Guilt must be atoned for in some way. Jesus took our guilt upon Himself as He gave His life on the cross. It was as if every blow hammering the nails in His hands was hammering nails into the coffin of our guilt.

For me, I have always had the tendency to carry false guilt—feeling responsible for things that turned out badly, whether or not I was really guilty. I hate conflict and I hate to disappoint others, so I would rather take the blame and apologize than wait for the guilty party to take responsibility. God has taught me that this is not a good way to be. I may be a stumbling block in God's bringing conviction to another person.

However, there are certainly times when truly I am guilty. What then? The only remedy for removing guilt is to confess my sin and receive God's forgiveness through my faith in His Son Jesus Christ. God loves us and longs for us to stand before Him guilt-free. There are also times when I confess, repent, and receive God's forgiveness but find it difficult to forgive myself. This is when I am greatly comforted by Romans 8:1. I have found that by meditating on this verse, emphasizing each word of the verse, I can feel reassured. The feelings catch up with the facts of my forgiveness. I can identify with the adulterous woman who was flung before Jesus. She might have told her story like this:

Free To Be

My life had been a hard one, and I was accustomed to being used by men, and then discarded as if I were just a piece of rubbish. But one day all of that changed. On that particular day, I had been dragged from the bed of my lover, only to be made a spectacle of in the Temple court. Though I was not religious, I knew what the Law said about adultery, and I knew I was guilty. Now, I thought, a sentence of stoning was about to be pronounced and carried out.

As I knelt there on the cold stones of the courtyard, head hung in shame, bracing myself for the worst, I began to sense there was something else going on. As the men had cruelly drug me into the courtyard, they had interrupted the teaching of a man called Jesus. I had heard rumors of this man. Some said He had performed miracles and was a great teacher. But I hadn't paid much attention. After all, he *was* a man, and to my mind, all men were alike—*not to be trusted!*

However, I was soon to find out this was no ordinary man. As I dared to raise my eyes a little to see my "judge," I saw something unique in this man's eyes. The purity I saw there only seemed to magnify my guiltiness. I cannot tell you how ashamed I felt—to be brought here to the temple, among all the religious people—and have my sin announced. Yet, in spite of the fact that I deserved condemnation, I saw in Jesus' eyes great compassion. As He bent down in the dirt and began to write, I was amazed, and so were my accusers. It looked as if He were writing down a list of sins. Soon, my accusers began to leave, one by one, from the oldest down to the youngest, and I was left standing alone before this Jesus. This Jesus, who had the power and authority to condemn, said to me: "Where are your accusers?

Does no one condemn you?" I answered, still awestruck: "No one, Lord."

Then He said the words that set me free—really free. He looked at me as no man had ever looked at me and said those beautiful, liberating words: "Neither do I condemn you." The words were so freeing for me that it was almost unnecessary for Him to remind me to "sin no more." Somehow His compassion reached deep inside me and made me want to turn from my sin. Here was a man who had stooped down to where I was—as if He were willing even to risk the stones' being hurled at Him. Here was a man willing to acknowledge the double standard of our day—for I wasn't the only one who had sinned. The same man who spoke words powerful enough to convict my accusers also spoke the gentle words my soul ached to hear—words of forgiveness. Is it any wonder that I came to acknowledge Him as the Messiah? Is it any wonder that I came to love Him and become one of His followers?

("The Adulterous Woman," monologue by Kay Coulter. Unpublished.)

Questions to Ponder

Question 1: Psalm 139:23-24 (KJV) says, " Search me, O God, and know my heart: try me, and know my thoughts: And see if there be any wicked way in me, and lead me in the way everlasting." Ask God to reveal to you those sins for which you are truly guilty.

Question 2: Are you carrying false guilt and condemning yourself unnecessarily?

Question 3: Have you placed your faith in Christ, and realized freedom from condemnation?

Memorize

Mark 16:16 (NIV)

"Whoever believes and is baptized will be saved, but whoever does not believe will be condemned."

NOTES

Day 21

Free from Self-righteousness

From the Dictionary

Self-righteousness: Noun - The quality or state of being self-righteous; pharisaism.

From the Word

Titus 3:4-6 (KJV)

> But after that the kindness and love of God our Saviour toward man appeared, not by works of righteousness which we have done, but according to his mercy he saved us, by the washing of regeneration, and renewing of the Holy Ghost; which he shed on us abundantly through Jesus Christ our Saviour.

Also read Luke 11:37-44; Matthew 9:16; Romans 3:10-18.

The opposite of self-righteousness is humility. We can gain real righteousness by recognizing our sinfulness and humbling ourselves before God. Jesus came to save sinners, not the righteous (in their own eyes). Righteousness comes to the one who expresses faith in Jesus, not to the one who thinks he is already good enough and deserves God's blessings. If we cannot depend on our own righteousness, then what does God require? Hosea 6:6 (NIV) says, "For I desire mercy, not sacrifice, and acknowledgment of God rather than burnt offerings." Much of God's displeasure with

His chosen people, the Jews, came from their hypocritical worship. They thought they were good enough to be accepted by God because they went through the rituals. Self-righteousness focuses on the external. It is easy to fall into the trap of self-righteousness if one goes through the motions—church attendance, singing hymns, serving on committees, etc. If the heart remains unchanged, it is all just empty ritual. Jesus condemned the hypocrisy of the religious leaders of His day—the Pharisees.

When one is wrapped in self-righteousness, he can become blind to his own sins. The Bible, however, makes it clear that no one is righteous on his own (See Romans 3:10-18). 1 Peter 4:17-18 tells us it is "hard for the righteous to be saved." The self-righteous person is only depending on himself—thinking he has something of worth to offer God. However, God says our righteousness is as "filthy rags" before Him (Isaiah 64:6). None of us can measure up to His standards of holiness.

The only antidote to the poison of self-righteous thinking is humility. In contrast to the "filthy rags" in which we clothe ourselves, Peter (1 Peter 5:5b-6) tells us to "clothe [our]selves in humility toward one another," because "God opposes the proud and gives grace to the humble." I would even suggest that if we don't humble ourselves before God, He will find ways to humble us. This has been true in my life. I used to have a real problem with self-righteousness. The cloak of self-righteousness served two purposes: (1) to be a defense measure to protect myself, covering up my insecurity; and (2) to give me a way to judge others. After all, I was not guilty of the "big" sins. Judging others became a way of separating myself from others who committed big sins—the murderers, homosexuals, Satan worshipers, and the like. The trouble with that is that Jesus has called us to be "salt" and "light," sharing the gospel of salvation with a dying world. How can we do this if we consider ourselves to be above others? Our judgment of them is not the "good news" they need to hear. When I look down on others, it is as if I have a watch by which everyone else should set their timepieces. How arrogant!

A current-day illustration of self-righteousness that condemns others is the attitude and actions of some in the Church who are preaching a message of hate. This is often racially motivated, but of late, what is in the news so much is the persecution against homosexuals. One particular event in the news that caught my attention was the controversy over a church group's desire to place a memorial in a park in Casper, Wyoming. This sounds benign enough, but get this! The memorial states "Matthew Shepard entered Hell, October 12, 1998." The case of Matthew Shepard made the news in 1998 because of the horror of his murder. He was a professing homosexual who certain residents of the town could not tolerate. Two men beat him up and left him tied to a fence post, where he suffered from hypothermia in zero-degree weather for five days before he died. Rightfully, the men who committed this horrible crime were convicted and sent to prison.

I remember at the time, I was sickened by this crime. This was a clear case of two men blinded by their unreasonable prejudice against one who was different from them. Another thing that disturbed me greatly was the presence of a pastor and some of his congregation who protested at the park across the street from the young man's funeral. This same group showed up five years later, seeking to place the above-mentioned memorial in a city park. Of course, the media hopped on this one! I saw where the pastor was interviewed, and I was appalled at his attitude and his faulty reasoning. He felt he needed to publicly condemn the victim for his homosexuality. Of course, he came across as a "gay-bashing homophobe." This man is a professing Christian, yet all I heard coming from his mouth was condemnation.

Where is the compassion that Christians are to exhibit? While I am certainly no proponent for sexual perversion and am very aware of the fact that God does condemn this sin (just as He condemns every sin you and I have committed), I don't believe we serve God's purposes by being identified with those who have an agenda of hate and prejudice. What are God's purposes? John 3:17 (NIV) says of Jesus' mission: "For God did not send his Son into the world to condemn the world, but to save the world through him."

We have a choice. We can hate those who are unlike us, carrying out God's judgment on our own, or we can be about the Father's business in sharing words of life to sinful mankind. Our self-righteousness is not going to save anybody, and in actuality, will turn many away from the Church. Our attitudes and actions need to be compassionate. Let us share the good news of the gospel of salvation that is available to all who confess Jesus as Savior and Lord, regardless of their sins. I leave you with this verse, "By this all men will know that you are my disciples, if you love one another" John 13:35 (NIV).

Questions to Ponder

Question 1: Do your words and actions reflect a hatred toward others who are unlike you?

Question 2: Do you categorize sin, differentiating between "big" sins and "little" sins?

Question 3: Are you actively pursuing the purposes of God?

Memorize

Romans 10:14-15 (NIV)

How, then, can they call on the one they have not believed in? And how can they believe in the one of whom they have not heard? And how can they hear without someone preaching to them? And how can they preach unless they are sent? As it is written, "How beautiful are the feet of those who bring good news!"

NOTES

Day 22

Free to Serve

From the Dictionary

Serve: Verb - Devote (part of) one's life or efforts to, as of countries, institutions, or ideas.

From the Word

Matthew 20:25-28 (NIV)

> Jesus called them together and said, "You know that the rulers of the Gentiles lord it over them, and their high officials exercise authority over them. Not so with you. Instead, whoever wants to become great among you must be your servant, and whoever wants to be first must be your slave—just as the Son of Man did not come to be served, but to serve, and to give his life as a ransom for many."

Also read: Hebrews 12:28; Matthew 25:14-30; Philippians 2:5-11.

"Servant" does not have a very positive connotation nowadays. Part of the American dream is that we will be affluent enough to be able to have servants who will serve us. A servant is even considered inferior in some circles and certainly is not a position for which one strives. Our whole concept of service is different from days gone by. For example, gone are the days when we actually received service at the gas pump. Remember when we called gas stations service stations? I remember pulling up to the pump and waiting for the attendant to pump the gas, clean the windshield, check the tires, and sometimes check the oil. It was great! I didn't even have to get out of the car. I got all this service for the price of gas, which was running around nineteen cents a gallon. This could have been a scene in the old Andy Griffith Show on TV, but the show did reflect real life in a small town.

This would not be so today, however, and has not been for a very long time now. Today, I drive up to the pump and serve myself, and if I want any of the other amenities, I do them myself. These self-serve pumps are symbolic of our "self-serve" society. We want what we want and we want it now! Self-gratification is a value that has deeply permeated our society. Even politicians who are supposed to be "public servants" are more interested in jockeying for positions of power and influence than in serving their constituents.

Contrast this societal mindset with the principles that Jesus taught His disciples. Jesus' followers are not to follow the ways of the world. We are to stand out from the crowd that is rushing headlong to destruction. From studying the words of Jesus and from apostolic teaching in the New Testament, we see both the attitudes about servanthood that should be characteristic of His followers and the rewards given for faithful service. First of all, there needs to be a humble heart and a grateful attitude, such as Paul expressed in 2 Timothy 1:3 (KJV): "I thank God, whom I serve from my forefathers with a pure conscience, that without ceasing I have remembrance of thee in my prayers night and day." Can you see how this servant attitude has permeated his being? It caused him:

- To be thankful;
- To have a clear conscience;
- To have a rich prayer life.

These three things, I believe, are foundational if we are to be free to serve. When we understand that we are free from the penalty of sin through God's grace, we can cease the striving which causes us to run roughshod over others. In humility, we recognize our sinfulness and that we are not above others. Gratitude rises out of humility.

Christ is our example in having a servant's spirit, as we can see in Philippians 2:5-11. What was His attitude about serving? We see from this passage and others that He served humbly, obediently, wholeheartedly, and joyfully. He even taught that in order to be great we must be willing to serve. Our ideas of greatness are in direction opposition to the plans of God. The one who would be greatest needs to be willing to be the least. First Peter 5:6 says, "Humble yourselves, therefore, under God's mighty hand, that he may lift you up in due time." Humility is the key to greatness.

What are the rewards of servanthood? Jesus taught several parables to illustrate genuine servanthood. What we see in these parables (i.e. the servants with the talents) is that there are rewards to those who serve God faithfully and condemnation for those who are just faking it. There are many among us who want to project an image of being Christians but they have not yet learned the meaning of servanthood. God expects us to give of ourselves freely and joyfully, and He will reward us according to His economy. It is true that much of our reward will come to us after we die and are in Heaven, and we can rejoice in knowing this. Nevertheless, much blessing comes to us in this life as well in the sense of satisfaction for a job well done, having our own needs furnished by God, the blessing of seeing others turn to Christ, and the freedom from striving.

Let us be faithful servants, for God has promised us that if we are faithful over a few things, He will allow us to rule over many things and we will enter the joy of the Lord (Matthew 25:21).

Questions to Ponder

Question 1: Would you describe your attitude as "striving" or "serving?"

Question 2: Are you seeking greatness? On what terms?

Question 3: Do you classify others according to the world's hierarchy?

Memorize
1 Peter 4:10

"Each one should use whatever gift he has received to serve others, faithfully administering God's grace in its various forms."

Free To Be

__NOTES__

Day 23

Free to Love

From the Dictionary

Agape: Noun – the highest and noblest form of love which sees something infinitely precious in its object.
(*The New Bible Dictionary,* Wm. B. Eerdmans Publishing Co., Grand Rapids, Michigan, 1962)

From the Word

John 13:34-35 (NIV)
"A new command I give you: Love one another. As I have loved you, so you must love one another. By this all men will know that you are my disciples, if you love one another."

Also read John 3:16; 1 John 3:1; 1 John 4:9; 19; Romans 5:8.

In the Gospels, we see the unfolding of Jesus' ministry on earth. We hear His teachings and see how His life demonstrated the truths that came from God. If we could with one word sum up Jesus' life and ministry on earth, that word would be "love." Out of His love for mankind, God sent His Son into the world to deliver us from our sinfulness. There is no way we could ever pay for our sins, so God provided the means to our salvation by sending His Son to die as a holy sacrifice. By placing our faith and trust in this sacrifice, we can experience God's agape love. We who believe are "infinitely precious" in His sight. It is in this context that we can truly experience unconditional love. Only when we have been wrapped up in the arms of God's love can we truly love others.

There is a promise in 1 John 4:18: "There is no fear in love. Perfect love casts out fear."

What is perfect love? Or better yet, who is the source of perfect love? 1 John 4:7a says, "Dear friends, let us love one another, for love comes from God." God is the source of love, for He *is* love. Love originates with Him. If you are seeking perfect love from any other source, you will be sorely disappointed. It is only the perfect love of God that enables us to overcome our fears.

When we are able to overcome our fears and feel secure in God's love, then we are free to love others as God loves them—with no strings attached. Jesus taught some pretty radical things when He instructed His followers concerning love. He said things like, "Love your enemies, do good to them, and lend to them without expecting to get anything back" Luke 6:35 (NIV). This kind of love is against our human nature. This is why it is so startling to the world that believers in Jesus can love this way. How can this be? It is only because of the work of God in our hearts. When we come to the realization that we have been forgiven for all our sins, we in turn can love and forgive others.

The kind of love that Jesus desires for His followers is essential for our well being and unity in the Church. When Jesus faced His last hours on earth—the mockery of a trial, the condemnation, the rejection, and finally, the crucifixion—He gave to His disciples the commandment to love each other. Their obedience to this teaching would be crucial in the future of the Church. Jesus knew He was about to be bodily taken from them and He was giving them instruction and comfort. He emphasized the need to love one another, knowing this in part would sustain them in a world where they would be rejected, scorned, and persecuted.

The Church serves the same purpose today. We as individuals are strengthened and encouraged by our fellow believers and their love for us when we go through various trials. The same John who wrote the gospel also wrote the epistles of 1, 2, and 3 John. First John especially is full of instructions to love. From this epistle we can see the following truths:

1) We are free to love unconditionally because of God's love for us.
2) Love is based on truth—honesty about who we are. We put ourselves in such bondage when we are not honest! Think of the honesty of a child—no hidden agenda, no hang-ups or prejudices. Being child-like (i.e. transparent) enables us to freely give of ourselves, loving others because we have nothing to hide.
3) Asking for God's forgiveness sets us free. We are no longer under the illusion that we are above others, for we have all sinned. By being honest about our sinfulness, we don't have to worry about keeping up an image.
4) We are secure in God's love, so we can be generous in our love toward others.
5) Love is dynamic—it expands as we draw closer to God and obey Him. In contrast, he who hates his brother is blinded, and the hatred blocks the love of God from moving through that person.

Jesus taught that God is love and that we love Him because He first loved us. In the two great commandments to love God and love others as ourselves, we see how the second is dependent on the first.

The world thinks it knows what love is about, but I contend that the world's definition of love is inadequate at best. The world's love has as its foundation selfishness—a "What's in it for me?" perspective. God's love is the filling station for those of us who love Him. Loving others means giving ourselves away. With regular visits to the Source of Love, I can be filled, enabling me to give love to others unconditionally.

Years ago, I read a book about God's economy. I have forgotten much of what the author wrote, but I remember the basic premise: what you need the most, be willing to give away. Free to love? Yes, we can freely give because we have freely received.

Questions to Ponder

Question 1: When you examine your heart, is there a blockage there of hatred, prejudice, or unforgiveness?

Question 2: Make a list of the attributes of God's love.

Memorize

1 Corinthians 13:4-7 (NIV)

> **"Love is patient, love is kind. It does not envy, it does not boast, it is not proud. It is not rude, it is not self-seeking, it is not easily angered, it keeps no record of wrongs. Love does not delight in evil but rejoices with the truth. It always protects, always trusts, always hopes, always perseveres."**

NOTES

Day 24

Free from Legalism

From the Dictionary

Legalism: Noun - Strict conformity to the letter of the law rather than its spirit.

From the Word

Galatians 3:10-11 (NIV)

> "All who rely on observing the law are under a curse, for it is written: "Cursed is everyone who does not continue to do everything written in the Book of the Law." Clearly no one is justified before God by the law, because, 'The righteous will live by faith.'"

Also read: Galatians 3:22-24; Ephesians 2:9-10; John 8:36; Romans 8:2

> *"I don't smoke, and I don't chew, and I don't go with the boys who do!"* This was a silly refrain I learned at the girls' camp that I attended when I was a child. Silly, yes, but it is somewhat symbolic of the legalistic mindset that has invaded the Church. Many times, Christians are identified more by the things they don't do than the things they do. Have you have heard statements like these?
> "I don't dance, I'm a Baptist."

"My church doesn't allow women to wear make-up or cut their hair."

"Women should not wear 'that which pertaineth to a man.'"

"I must go to my priest for confession."

"The Sacraments of the Church are what save you."

"We are not allowed to use musical instruments in our church."

The legalistic and traditional rules and rituals we impose upon ourselves run the gamut from the silly to the sublime. When I was a young married woman, my church sent out sixty of its members on a mission trip to Mexico. During the day, we conducted Vacation Bible Schools in three locations in the town, and had some free time in the evenings. I remember that one lady, the oldest member of our group, refused as a matter of principle to play cards during our recreational time, and she really criticized those who chose to do so. However, she thought it was all right to play dominoes. What kind of religious standard is that? Could it be the Pharisaical standard of hypocrisy? Unfortunately, some of the legalism is not harmless, such as whether to play cards or not. Many believe their salvation and right standing with God depend on their rule-keeping ability. They completely miss the wonderful gift of God's grace, which is offered to us not because we deserve it but because of Christ's sacrifice on the cross. He was the only one who could meet the standards that a holy God demanded as a sacrifice for sin.

Paul teaches through his epistles from the authority as an apostle given him by Christ. He who was once very zealous for the traditions long held by the Pharisees was delivered from them and set free to live according to grace. His conversion experience even demonstrates this. As he was living in the "old man," he was on his way to persecute the despised Christians. He thought he was doing the right thing. After all, he was religious and thought he was doing what God wanted him to do! However, when he met Jesus on the road to Damascas, he was struck blind. His physical blindness, I believe, was a symbol of the spiritual blinders that had characterized him. By rejecting the Gospel message of salvation through Christ, he took on the spiritual blindness of the very ones Jesus had condemned—those who elevated tradition above the Word of God. They were blind to the fact that Jesus fulfilled all the prophecies concerning their Messiah. They settled for second best by adhering to the Law, not realizing they could be free from the requirements of the Law by placing their trust in the Messiah Jesus Christ.

This kind of faith in the Messiah is the only thing that can save us. No works of the Law or manmade traditions can free us from the shackles of sin. Although God has clearly communicated this truth through His inspired Word, even today there are many who want to cling to the myth that we can earn our salvation by performing rituals and living according to legalistic requirements. In his book, *Real Christians Don't Dance* (with a slash mark through the "Don't"), John Fischer states: "Modern Christianity has gravitated to a list of *do's* and *don'ts* because this spells out the distinctiveness so clearly. Being born again becomes a simple matter of following a prescribed formula" (p. 16, 1988: Minneapolis, MN: Bethany House Publishers). The book goes on to point out the silliness of some traditions and the sidestepping of the real Gospel message.

There are people who are false believers and false teachers who would try to deceive us and take away our freedom in Christ (Galatians 2:4). We need to resist the teaching that would cause us to rely on legalistic or ritualistic rules in order to secure our salvation and right standing before God.

Even dedicated Christians can be led astray if we are not careful. In Galatians, Paul mentions the case of Peter, Barnabas, and other Jewish Christians who were afraid to embrace fully the freedom of Christ in relating to Gentile Christians. They feared criticism from the Judaizers, so they withdrew from fellowship with the Gentiles. The whole book of Galatians challenges believers to avoid this kind of behavior. The Galatian believers had gotten caught up in believing that they needed more than faith in order to know God and have salvation. Again and again, Paul points out that it is not by human efforts that we are made right with God. The Law, for them, consisted of the stated laws of God given to Moses plus the hundreds of laws imposed upon them by a corrupted priesthood. Paul wanted the Galatians to know the freedom they could have in Christ.

We who are believers today need to heed the inspired words God spoke through Paul. It is only through faith in Christ that we have the promise of the Spirit, of salvation, of eternal life and of abundant life. Many within the Church today, however, want to insist on adding requirements which become heavy burdens. Think of it! Every denomination has its false teachers who would impose their legalism on us with teachings that regulate what we eat and drink, what we wear, how we use the spiritual gifts (i.e. tongues-speaking), how we worship (contemporary or traditional), and how we can gain favor with God by our good works. These things are taught in such a way as to cause a believer to think that he is not saved or not spiritual enough. This is bondage. Christ came to set us free!

Does that mean we can live any way we choose? No, but our salvation (our right standing with God) does not depend on the external things. When we fully realize there is no requirement of the Law or legalistic standard set by another person that can save us and give us new life, then we are humbled before God. It is in our humility of heart (not pride in what we can do) that God can use us to be "ministers of reconciliation" to a dying world. Let us stop our legalistic game-playing, which brings God's condemnation, and be released to enjoy our freedom in Christ. Remember, the world is waiting to hear the Good News, not about our spiritual superiority.

Questions to Ponder

Question 1: Can you think of an example of legalistic teaching in your church or denomination?

Question 2: In examining your lifestyle, would you say you live more by Scripture or by tradition?

Memorize

Galatians 3:23-25 (NIV)

"Before this faith came, we were held prisoners by the law, locked up until faith should be revealed. So the law was put in charge to lead us to Christ that we might be justified by faith. Now that faith has come, we are no longer under the supervision of the law. "

NOTES

Day 25

The Power Released

From the Dictionary

Power: Noun – Possession of the qualities (especially mental qualities) required to do something or get something done.

From the Word

Ephesians 3:14-21 (NIV)

> For this reason I kneel before the Father, from whom his whole family in heaven and on earth derives its name I pray that out of his glorious riches he may strengthen you with power through his Spirit in your inner being, so that Christ may dwell in your hearts through faith. And I pray that you, being rooted and established in love, may have power, together with all the saints, to grasp how wide and long and high and deep is the love of Christ, and to know this love that surpasses knowledge—that you may be filled to the measure of all the fullness of God.
>
> Now to him who is able to do immeasurably more than all we ask or imagine, according to his power that is at work within us, to him be glory in the church and in Christ Jesus throughout all generations, for ever and ever! Amen.

Also read 1 Peter 5:8-11; 1 John 5:5.

It is a natural human desire to have power and authority. I believe God put this desire in our hearts in His creation of us. However, He has also given us much guidance from the Word in the proper use of the power that comes from Him. From Genesis (creation of Adam) to Revelation (victorious return of Christ), we see great displays of God's power, as well as how He empowered His people to overcome great obstacles in their life journeys.

There is a right use of power and a wrong use of power. Much of the wreckage of human life can be traced to the misuse of power. Unredeemed mankind thirsts for power that will enable us to control others for our own selfish ambitions. Power gained by selfish and self-centered means is used only for the benefit of the one wielding it. Because of the misuse of power, history is littered with the debris of fallen empires, disenfranchised and persecuted peoples, heinous acts of evil, and broken lives.

As Christians, we must not buy into the world's idea of "personal power." When Jesus walked this earth, His teachings were both revolutionary and paradoxical, and they have lived on through His apostles. His very words have power! What did He have to say about power? In many cases, it was just the opposite of what we want to hear! He said things like:

> He that findeth his life shall lose it: and he that loseth his life for my sake shall find it.
> Matthew 10:39 (KJV)

> But he that is greatest among you shall be your servant. Matthew 23:11 (KJV)

> Humble yourselves, therefore, under God's mighty hand, that he may lift you up in due time. 1 Peter 5:6 (NIV)

> For God hath not given us the spirit of fear; but of

power, and of love, and of a sound mind. 2 Timothy 1:7 (KJV)

The one who is in you is greater than the one who is in the world. 1 John 4:4 (NIV)

Jesus was saying that real power is not something to be grasped, but rather it is given by grace to those who seek to follow God and submit to His Lordship. Paul, in his letter to the Ephesians, prayed that they would experience the liberating power of the Holy Spirit. This power would be evidenced in the inner man. Paul's prayer for the Ephesians reveals to us these truths about God-given power:

1. The source is God's glorious riches – an unlimited supply.
2. Faith in Jesus Christ is essential.
3. The foundation is love – this love will keep us from misusing power.
4. The power given from above is intended to help us grow in our relationship with Christ, and it unlocks the storehouse of love He has for us.
5. The power of His love surpasses knowledge – it is not just something we acknowledge in our minds but power that we experience in our hearts, even to "the measure of all the fullness of God."
6. The power from above is to be used to build up the church.
7. His power within will enable us to endure through times of trial and persecution.
8. The power we are given through Christ will enable us to glorify Him.

Do you want power? Then plug into the Source, who generously gives to us that we might overcome the world.

Questions to Ponder

Question 1: What is the power that you seek?

Question 2: In times of powerlessness and helplessness, where do you go for help?

Question 3: Compare the power of the world and the power that comes from God.

Memorize

2 Peter 1:3 (NIV)

"His divine power has given us everything we need for life and godliness through our knowledge of him who called us by his own glory and goodness."

NOTES

Day 26

Escape!

From the Dictionary

Free: Adjective – Not taken up by scheduled activities.

From the Word

Psalms 55:6 (NIV)

> "I said, "Oh, that I had the wings of a dove! I would fly away and be at rest—I would flee far away and stay in the desert; Selah. I would hurry to my place of shelter, far from the tempest and storm."

Also read Psalm 16:9; Psalm 62:5; Matthew 11:28-30.

We live in a day and time that finds us ever stretching our physical, mental, and emotional resources. Americans are prone to overachieving, competing with others on the ladder of success, making ourselves available for every whim of our children, and just generally being busy. As a result we are washed out, burned out, worn out, and spiritually drained. It is as if we have decided that the problems of the world rest on our shoulders, and we feel guilty if we are not always doing something.

What do you think is the reason for all this hustle-bustle activity? Could it be that we do not want to take time to be reflective? For if we do, then we must think about things like: "What is my purpose in life?"

"What are my inner resources?"
"Are my choices of lifestyle affecting my health?"
"How do I relate to others?"
"What is God's will?"

I read an article recently that purported the benefits of meditation for bodily healing. There also have been studies done in the medical field showing that prayer is beneficial for patients and speeds their healing. Isn't it interesting in our culture that prayer and meditation are a "discovery?" We do not have to rely on our culture for wisdom in this area, however, for the Bible speaks much about the need for rest, meditation on Scripture, and prayer. I would even dare to say that our very lives depend on it. We just need to escape from the pressures of our world from time to time.

David expressed his desire to have "the wings of a dove" so that he could "fly away and be at rest." Do you ever feel this way? I certainly do. Sometimes the stress of circumstances, ill health, and bearing burdens (both my own and others') start piling up on me, and I really feel the need to pull away, get in a quiet place without distractions, and renew my resources. When I do, I not only feel less stressed but I also begin to feel God's peace encompass me. I am brought to the place where I can evaluate my words and actions to see if I have displeased God by offending others or ignoring the needs of those who require my presence. God said in Psalm 46:10, "Be still, and know that I am God." It is in stillness of body and spirit that we can realize His work in our lives—how we are growing spiritually and how we are influencing others.

We need to be free from the cares of the world, and sometimes the only way to experience that freedom is to take time off, go to a quiet place and just commune with God. He has opened the door to let us into His presence by sending Jesus to be our Savior. Through Jesus we can experience the rest—physical and spiritual—that God intends for our well being. Whether it be an occasional retreat or just our day-to-day quiet times with the Lord, we can rest in His presence and have our souls restored. Let us "fly like a dove" in our spirits to the shelter of God's everlasting arms.

Questions to Ponder

Question 1: What activities in your life keep you from experiencing God's rest?

Question 2: Is there a place to which you can go to escape the daily pressures of life?

Question 3: If you don't already have a quiet time set aside, make an appointment with yourself, keep it, and list ways this benefits you.

Memorize

Matthew 11:29 (NIV)
"Take my yoke upon you and learn from me, for I am gentle and humble in heart, and you will find rest for your souls."

NOTES

Day 27

Free from Falsehood

From the Dictionary

Truth: Noun - Conformity to reality or actuality.

From the Word

John 8:32 (KJV)

> "And ye shall know the truth, and the truth shall make you free."

Also read Psalm 51:6; Ephesians 4:25; 1 John 4:6; John 3:21

What is it about truth that sets us free? Does this verse imply that if we are not living in truth that we are in bondage? I think it does. I have met a number of people who are deceivers and the ones that they deceive the most are themselves. This truly is bondage, for it is much harder to maintain a life that is built on lies. The more that one believes the lies, the less able he is to see the truth when confronted with it. I am sure you know some people whom you do not trust because you never know when they are telling the truth. This is because they have established a pattern of lying that characterizes them. It is a sad sight to see, for this kind of person cuts himself off from meaningful relationships. The main relationship that is hindered, of course, is with God. It is only when we come to be truthful with ourselves about who and what we are that we are truly free to enter into a relationship with God.

The Psalmist David recognized this truth when he penned the words, "Surely you desire truth in the inner parts; you teach me wisdom in the inmost place" (Psalms 51:6). This revelation came to him when he was confronted by Nathan the Prophet concerning his sins of adultery and murder. This great chapter of Psalms reveals much about David, "a man after God's own heart." We see his willingness to look into his own heart, acknowledge the sinfulness that was there, and repent, asking God for forgiveness. After he did this, he was set free—free to enjoy a wonderful relationship with God and to know His blessings upon him.

I remember when I came to the realization that I was in need of inner healing. God brought to my mind some latent memories of abuse that I had suffered as a child. He provided a counselor who prayed me through some very difficult encounters in my past. At first, I was somewhat skeptical about the whole idea of hidden (repressed) memories and inner healing, but as I began to pray and seek God's will in this matter, I was led to His Word for the answers. One of the key scriptures that helped me was Psalm 51:6. I came to realize I had been in denial about my past for many years, but in my thirties, I saw that God had prepared me to deal with the victimization I had experienced as a child. As I looked at my past with the desire to know the truth, God helped me begin my healing journey.

Truth! Why is it so important? We live in a society where truth is not highly regarded. There are philosophers who say truth is relative—meaning, I suppose, they do not want to be held accountable to someone else's idea of truth. We so easily excuse ourselves with "little white lies," cheating on income tax and expense reports, disobeying traffic laws, etc. This disregard for the truth becomes a slippery slope that leads to the erosion of our integrity.

Does it really matter? Yes! Do you remember that Jesus

called Himself "the Way, the Truth, and the Life"? He is THE TRUTH. He personifies truth and He is the one from whom we can know whether or not we are living in truth. It is He who leads us in looking into our "inner parts." We are called to be children of light, making us approachable, transparent, and genuine in our relationships with others. Nobody likes a phony or a hypocrite. If we who follow Christ are not truthful, how are we going to draw others to Christ?

This matter of truthfulness is very important indeed. Ephesians 4:25 says, "Therefore each of you must put off falsehood and speak truthfully to his neighbor." In John 3:21, Jesus emphasizes the importance of truthfulness: "But whoever lives by the truth comes into the light, so that it may be seen plainly that what he has done has been done through God."

Not only should we speak the truth to others, we must be truthful with ourselves. That means that we cannot deny that we are sinners. It is as if we take a magnifying glass (which we love to use on others!) and hold it over our own hearts. This allows God's Spirit to do His work of convicting us of any hidden sin. It is easy to shove aside bad attitudes such as bitterness, unforgiveness, pride and anger, but we need to be free from these things, not clutch them to us as if they define who we are.

This book has spoken of many things from which we can be free, but this freedom can only come when we are willing to be truthful with ourselves. It takes courage, but God supplies this in ample amounts when we come before him in humility, being honest about our shortcomings. From there we can truly experience freedom for as we "...walk in the light, as he is in the light, we have fellowship with one another, and the blood of Jesus, his Son, purifies us from all sin" (1 John 1:7).

Questions to Ponder

Question 1: Can you think of some ways that you have been dishonest?

Question 2: Is there someone you do not trust because of his lack of integrity?

Question 3: List the benefits of being truthful.

Memorize

1 John 1:6-7

> **"If we claim to have fellowship with him yet walk in the darkness, we lie and do not live by the truth. But if we walk in the light, as he is in the light, we have fellowship with one another, and the blood of Jesus, his Son, purifies us from all sin."**

Free To Be

<u>NOTES</u>

Day 28

Free from Pride

From the Dictionary

Pride: Noun – Unreasonable and inordinate self-esteem (personified as one of the deadly sins)

From the Word

Proverbs 16:18

> "Pride goes before destruction, a haughty spirit before a fall."

Romans 12:3

> "For by the grace given me I say to every one of you: Do not think of yourself more highly than you ought, but rather think of yourself with sober judgment, in accordance with the measure of faith God has given you."

Also read Proverbs 29:23; 2 Corinthians 5:12, 7:4, 8:24; Philippians 2:8

Why should we need to be free from pride? Is pride not a good thing? Don't I have a right to be proud of my accomplishments, proud of my children, etc.? Well, that depends. First of all we need to know what the Bible has to say about pride.

In Proverbs we see that pride is portrayed as being

negative, warning us that "pride goes before destruction, a haughty spirit before a fall." This kind of pride is arrogance and it leads one to feel superior to others. In adopting this attitude as a mindset, the proud person sets himself up for a fall. Humility does the opposite—it lifts up a man (Proverbs 29:23).

We have an oft-repeated phrase in our society. It is the concept of the "self-made man." This is descriptive of a person who thinks he has succeeded in reaching a goal on his initiative alone. I take issue with this concept. No person succeeds without the help of others (parents, coworkers, teachers, etc.) and if he/she thinks so, he/she is blind and arrogant. Ultimately, true success comes from the Lord, and if you want "bragging rights," then brag on Him. It is He who gives us life, strength, health, abilities, wisdom—the building blocks of life.

The New Testament sheds more light on the negative aspect of pride. We are admonished to "not be proud, but be willing to associate with people of low position. Do not be conceited" (Romans 12:16). We are told that love is not proud and does not boast in itself (1 Corinthians 13:4). In his epistle, James tells us in 4:6 that, "God opposes the proud." That last statement alone is enough reason to avoid improper pride (arrogance, conceit, self-centeredness). In interpreting the meaning of Proverbs 16:18, Life Application Bible Notes (Bible Explorer 3.0, Copyright 2003, WORDsearch Standard Edition) says:

> Proud people take little account of their weaknesses and do not anticipate stumbling blocks. They think they are above the frailties of common people. In this state of mind they are easily tripped up. Ironically, proud people seldom realize that pride is their problem, although everyone around them is well aware of it. Ask someone you trust whether self-satisfaction has blinded you to warning signs.

Free To Be

He or she may help you avoid a fall.

Is there a positive kind of pride? Yes, this concept is in Scripture also. Paul, in writing to the Corinthians, expressed a desire for that body of believers to take pride in him (as he had been faithful to share the Gospel) and not to take pride in superficial things (money, popularity, status). These were the things that the false teachers were practicing and were drawing some away from true faith. In turn, he says he "takes pride in" the Corinthians, a pride that speaks of confidence in others and is based on love (2 Corinthians 2:3-4). He states his devotion to them in verse 3, assuring them that he has their best interests at heart. This is the kind of pride we can feel for our children, as well as for friends and acquaintances whom we are encouraging, such as Paul was doing with the fledgling Corinthian Church.

> I have great confidence in you; I take great pride in you. I am greatly encouraged; in all our troubles my joy knows no bounds. 2 Corinthians 7:4

Paul admonishes us to have a balanced view of ourselves, neither too high nor too low. He says in the Romans passage listed above that we are to "think of [ourselves] with sober judgment." The long-respected theologian Matthew Henry sheds light on this verse and the meaning of "sober." We are not to over inflate our egos, but neither are we to put ourselves down.

> We must not say, I am nothing, therefore I will sit still, and do nothing; but, I am nothing in myself, and therefore I will lay out myself to the utmost, in the strength of the grace of Christ. (Matthew Henry Concise—Bible Explorer 3.0, Copyright 2003)

Pride can be dangerous, not only in our relationships with others but also in our relationship with God as well. I have experienced first-hand the matter of having a "haughty spirit" that comes before a fall. It was not a terribly traumatic event, but I learned the lesson God was trying to teach me. I used to walk for exercise at the local mall, and one day as I was making my rounds, I noticed something odd; but first let me describe my attitude that day. I had bought a new outfit that I really liked (leopard print top and black pants) and had worn it that day. I was really feeling spiffy in my new garb and congratulated myself on my shopping expertise. At the time, I was speaking and singing for audiences across the United States and I was very aware of my "image." Now it was important for me to look good (after all, I didn't want to look like a slob on stage!), but I am afraid I got a little carried away with placing my "image" as a priority. Anyway, as I was walking around the mall, I could not help but notice my reflection in the store windows along the way. I had already made several laps and I thought, "Oh, Kay, you're lookin' good!"

Now when a woman wears a new outfit, she likes to hear compliments. (Let's face it, we are naturally inclined to this stroking of our egos!) However, instead of receiving compliments, I felt embarrassed. When I glanced to my right and caught my reflection in a window, I noticed something hanging on my backside. *"What is that?"* I wondered. As I twisted around to see what was making this "tail," I was mortified to see that it was a black sock! As soon as I noticed my unwanted appendage, I quickly released it from its state of static cling and jammed it into my pants pocket. The next few minutes of walking had me wondering if anyone else had seen me. I thought, *"Oh dear, what if someone I know has seen me, or worse yet, someone I do not know has seen and is laughing at me behind my back."* The panic of worrying about my "image" quickly dissipated, however, and my funny bone kicked in. The more I thought about it, the funnier it became. The laughter helped me not

Free To Be

---

to take myself so seriously in an inconsequential matter. Then I began to see the lesson God was trying to teach me about pride. I had been giving too much attention to the external, giving it prominence over the internal. I realized that if we are to take pride in anything, we should first take pride in God (as Paul did when he said in 1 Corinthians 1:31, "Let him who boasts boast in the Lord").

Questions to Ponder

Question 1: Have you ever thought about both the negative and positive characteristics of pride?

Question 2: Has there ever been a time when God showed you that you have exhibited improper and destructive pride?

Memorize

Philippians 2:3-4

> **"Do nothing out of selfish ambition or vain conceit, but in humility consider others better than yourselves. Each of you should look not only to your own interests, but also to the interests of others."**

NOTES

Day 29

Things From Which We Cannot Be Free

From the Dictionary

Trial: Noun - An annoying or frustrating or catastrophic event

From the Word

James 1:2-4 (NIV)

> Consider it pure joy, my brothers, whenever you face trials of many kinds, because you know that the testing of your faith develops perseverance. Perseverance must finish its work so that you may be mature and complete, not lacking anything.

Also read Romans 5:1-4; Hebrews 12:1-12, 13:5; 1 Peter 1:6-7, 5:7.

In reading the title of this lesson you may be thinking, "Wait a minute! I thought this book was about freedom. You mean, God does not set us free from everything?" The answer is "No," because there are things on this earth from which we cannot be free. I am sure if you stopped to think a little, you would think of several things. This lesson is designed to help you think on the things from which we cannot be free.

One of the first things that comes to my mind is *disappointment*. Others will disappoint us and we will disappoint ourselves. Whenever our expectations are not met, we open ourselves to disappointment. I once attended a seminar in which the speaker brought up this subject. His advice to us was something like this: "Have no expectations and you won't be disappointed." Well, that may sound good, but in reality it is impossible not to have expectations. The important thing to learn from disappointments is that we have an opportunity to grow in our faith. There is only One in whom we will not be disappointed, as it says in Romans 5:5, "And hope does not disappoint us, because God has poured out his love into our hearts by the Holy Spirit, whom he has given us."

Another thing from which we cannot be free is *failure*. We cannot be error-free in this life, for we are all frail humans. Some of the ways in which we will fail include:
1. Always being right
2. Loving unconditionally all the time
3. Accomplishing all we want to accomplish

The question is not "Will I fail?" but rather "What is my response to failure?" There is a maxim common to our society that says, "If at first you don't succeed, try, try again." The reality is, however, that there are times we will not succeed no matter how many times we try, particularly in relationships. We may fail to win the love and admiration and respect for which we long. Building relationships takes at least two people committed to the process. Though we may fail in our relationships with others, we can know beyond the shadow of a doubt that God will not fail us and that He is always near. Remember His promise in Hebrews 13:5b, "Never will I leave you; never will I forsake you."

Another thing from which we cannot escape in this life is *criticism*. Now, I have the personality type that really cringes at others' criticisms. I have a tendency to want to please everyone, and I strive to do my best at every endeavor so that I will win approval by people who are important to me. I like to avoid pain and, let's face it—criticism is just plain painful! Different people will react differently to criticism (some expect it, some are challenged by it, some fear it, some laugh it off), but it is something we have to deal with as long as we walk this earth. What did Jesus have to say about criticism? "Blessed are you when people insult you, persecute you and falsely say all kinds of evil against you because of me. Rejoice and be glad, because great is your reward in heaven, for in the same way they persecuted the prophets who were before you" (Matthew 5:11-12 NIV).

Now, granted, we do not always receive criticism because of our faith. What about the critical words haunting us that are petty and pointless? A wise person once taught me the way to handle criticism. She advises to listen politely to the one criticizing you, thank him for their concern, and then give yourself time to reflect on what was said. For the ways in which you are truly wrong, set about correcting your words or actions, and seek God's forgiveness. If, in reflecting, you discover the criticism to be unwarranted, then just discard it, holding no ill feelings toward to the bearer of bad news. As a public speaker, I have found this method of dealing with criticism to be quite helpful. Of course, it is harder to practice this with ones we love, but when relationships are at stake, it is always better to favor the relationship over any perceived offense. We can draw some comfort also from these words of Jesus, knowing that He suffered greatly on our behalf: "If the world hates you, keep in mind that it hated me first. If you belonged to the world, it would love you as its own. As it is, you do not belong to the world, but I have chosen you out of the world. That is why the world hates you" (John 15:18-19 NIV).

There are many other things that came to my mind from which we cannot be free, such as temptation, sinning, sorrow, etc. I am sure you can think of others, but I will just fit the rest of these things into the general category of *trials*. The Bible has much to say about the sufferings of God's people. In the Old Testament, we see the sufferings of the Jews, most of which they brought on themselves because of their disobedience. Since the time of Christ's coming to earth, Christians have suffered greatly. The Bible clearly states that followers of Jesus Christ will suffer trials. It is hard to understand the teaching of some in our day who say that God only wants to shower us with blessings (health and wealth). God is interested in refining us and perfecting our faith. He does this by allowing us to experience trials in order that we will learn to trust Him. If we are honest, we have to admit that in times when everything is going well, we tend to forget from whose hands these blessings come; but as soon as we enter another time of trial, we turn to God for help. This is the place where God wants us—close to Him, dependent on Him for our every need, trusting His provision for this life and the next.

The next life is the one without trials. If we have faith in Christ, we are promised an eternity of living free from *disappointment, criticism, failure,* and *trials* of all kinds. How we respond to trials in this life will prepare us for life in heaven, because we will be rewarded for our faithfulness. The only place to test our faithfulness is here on this earth. So, let me encourage you to "Humble yourselves, therefore, under God's mighty hand, that he may lift you up in due time. Cast all your anxiety on him because he cares for you" (1 Peter 5:6-7 NIV). Let us look forward together to the time when we will live with the Father in a place that is truly free of pain and suffering, and where Jesus reigns in all His glory, for "every knee shall bow to me, and every tongue shall confess to God" (Romans 14:11 KJV).

Questions to Ponder

Question 1: Are there circumstances in your life in which you have not "cast all your care" upon the Lord?

Question 2: Do you look for God's lessons in the midst of trials?

Question 3: Are you growing in your faith and in your faithfulness?

Memorize

1 Corinthians 10:13 (NIV)

> **"No temptation has seized you except what is common to man. And God is faithful; he will not let you be tempted beyond what you can bear. But when you are tempted, he will also provide a way out so that you can stand up under it."**

NOTES

Day 30

Grace—Free But Not Cheap

From the Dictionary

Free: Adjective – Costing nothing

From the Word

Romans 5:8-11 (KJV)

> But God commendeth his love toward us, in that, while we were yet sinners, Christ died for us. Much more then, being now justified by his blood, we shall be saved from wrath through him. For if, when we were enemies, we were reconciled to God by the death of his Son, much more, being reconciled, we shall be saved by his life. And not only *so*, but we also joy in God through our Lord Jesus Christ, by whom we have now received the atonement.

Hebrews 2:9

> "But we see Jesus, who was made a little lower than the angels, now crowned with glory and honor because he suffered death, so that by the grace of God he might taste death for everyone."

Also read Isaiah 53; Luke 23:6-49; Philippians 2:5-11

It is an awesome thought to ponder the cost of grace. It is not of any cost to us, but it cost Jesus everything as He willingly gave up his life on the cross. Think with me for a few moments about what it cost Him. In the hours leading up to Jesus' arrest, He tried desperately to help his disciples understand that He was not the Messiah who would come and destroy the Roman government, as most Jews in His day believed. Instead, He would be taken captive by that government and look to all the world like a failure as a Messiah. The soldiers and spectators would mock him, saying, "You who are going to destroy the temple and build it in three days, save yourself! Come down from the cross, if you are the Son of God!" (Matthew 27:40 NIV). He must have suffered great mental agony as He thought about what was coming. The heaviness of this truth lay upon His heart. As He gathered with the disciples at the last Passover supper, He used the occasion to say goodbye to them, knowing that they would all desert Him in His hour of need. Imagine what it must have been like to have this knowledge. These were the men with whom He had lived and walked, with whom He had shared a ministry for three years that stretched across Israel from Galilee in the north to Judea in the South. They had had many good times of sharing as they witnessed miracles and listened to His teaching. He taught them how to live. He was Life itself. Now He would teach them how to die. Indeed, the agony of saying goodbye weighed heavily upon Him. He had to let the earthly relationships go in order to provide for them a heavenly relationship with the Father.

Then, of course, there was the one disciple who would not only desert Him but would also be the betrayer who delivered Him into the hands of those who wanted to kill Him. I wonder what Jesus must have felt, knowing that Judas would betray Him. He could have stopped this madness all along, but instead He marched resolutely toward the cross in order to fulfill prophecy and do the will of the Father. We know that Jesus had a great sense of purpose regarding His suffering, but that does not mean that it was not painful for Him. The mental pain and emotional anguish was almost more than He could bear, but He chose to bear it for our sakes as well as those who had been close to Him on this earth.

His agony is shown vividly in His prayer in the garden of Gethsemane. The Scriptures tell us that He "was overwhelmed with sorrow to the point of death" (Matthew 26:38). Can you imagine the intensity of the prayer that would cause Him to sweat, as it were, great drops of blood? He knew that He could escape the pain and agony, for if He called on God to send thousands of angels to help Him, God would do it. However, He chose to bear the mental anguish and emotional pain and gave His will over to the Father's purposes.

When He was taken from the Garden of Gethsemane to stand before His accusers, a mockery of a trial proceeded. Though nearly everything about the trial was illegal according to Jewish law, His accusers (the *religious leaders*) would still have their way. He had to endure their questioning and their false accusations as well as endure physical abuse, as they spat in His face, struck Him with their fists and slapped Him. This was just the beginning of the physical torture that He would have to endure. In addition to this, He would have to see the denial of Peter, one of His closest friends.

He was bound and sent to Pilate, the spineless government official who, even knowing this man was innocent, gave in to the cry of the crowds to crucify Him. Crucifixion was truly one of the worst, if not *the* worst, punishments devised by man. It hurts me to think of the physical suffering that came to Jesus as He was beaten with a staff, mocked by the soldiers, stripped of His clothes, spat upon by both the soldiers and the passersby. We can only imagine what the pain must have been like to be nailed to the cross—

to have large iron stakes driven through His hands and feet and a spear thrust through His side. Worst of all, He was *forsaken by God*. All this He willingly took on for one reason only—to be the sacrificial lamb who would secure our salvation from sin. The religious leaders of the Jews and the Roman government are not the only ones accountable for His death, for you and I must also take responsibility. Our sins put Him on that cross. Jesus' suffering and ultimate resurrection allowed God to offer us the free gift of grace, forgiveness, love, and eternal life. There is nothing we can do nor price that we can pay for this gift.

There is, however, a cost to us for following Jesus. This is the cost of discipleship. What are we willing to pay in terms of standing for our faith, living righteous lives, and giving of our resources as we participate in God's Kingdom work? American Christians have had it easy, for the most part. We have not been called upon to suffer for our faith like the multitudes of Christians in other lands. The day may come, however, when we will face persecution and loss. It behooves us to reflect on this possibility so that we can be ready when it comes. I ponder this possibility from time to time, and I wonder if I will be able to hold to my faith when faced with the demand that I renounce Christ. Jesus knew that the early Christians would indeed face persecution, torture, and death by holding on to their faith, but He promised that the Holy Spirit would strengthen them through the fiery trials. I have to believe that He will do this for me as well.

I remember vividly a play I was in at one time. It was a musical drama called "Joy Comes in the Morning" and I played the role of Mary, the mother of Jesus. The play included the crucifixion scene and, as Mary, it was necessary for me to be a part of it. The scene opened with the Roman soldiers bringing Christ in and placing him on the cross. I then entered and knelt at the foot of the cross, where

I was to respond to what was happening and then sing a song. I do not remember now what my lines were or even what the song was, but I will never forget looking at "my son" on the cross. Even knowing that it was just a drama—the blood on his body and the agony on his face not real—I was totally enthralled by what I saw. I truly took on the character of Mary and felt what she must have felt. At the time, I had a grown son, so it was easy for me to imagine this mother/son relationship and to feel Mary's pain. God spoke to me in that moment, making me realize the suffering of Jesus my Savior in a way I had not known before.

Many times I have gone back in my mind to that scene, and I am always humbled at the thought of Jesus' great gift of grace. Oh how I want to be found faithful! I owe Him everything and I desire to be willing to pay the cost of discipleship, whatever that may be. Jesus taught, "Whoever finds his life will lose it, and whoever loses his life for my sake will find it" (Matthew 10:39 NIV). Paul, in his epistle to the Colossians (1:10-14), amplifies the meaning of what it means to lose my life for Christ's sake:

> And we pray this in order that you may live a life worthy of the Lord and may please him in every way: bearing fruit in every good work, growing in the knowledge of God, being strengthened with all power according to his glorious might so that you may have great endurance and patience, and joyfully giving thanks to the Father, who has qualified you to share in the inheritance of the saints in the kingdom of light. For he has rescued us from the dominion of darkness and brought us into the kingdom of the Son he loves, in whom we have redemption, the forgiveness of sins.

Questions

Question 1: With whom do you identify in the crucifixion of Jesus—the deniers; the believers; the deserters; the betrayers; the killers?

Question 2: Have you ever sacrificed in order to be a follower of Christ? What is the personal cost to you?

Memorize

Romans 5:8 (NIV)

> **"But God demonstrates his own love for us in this: While we were still sinners, Christ died for us."**

NOTES

A Final Word from the Author

This last chapter was difficult for me to write—for two reasons. I do not like looking at the ugliness of the crucifixion and how Jesus suffered, and also I am challenged (just as the Word challenges you, dear reader) to think of the sacrifices I am willing to make in order to follow Christ. I consider myself to be on the journey to mature faith just like my readers. The different aspects of freedom that I cover in this book are something that I have experienced in my struggles to allow God to conform me to the image of His Son Jesus Christ. It is my prayer that you, the reader, will join me on this journey to personal freedom that we might learn to live, love, worship, and serve extravagantly. Let us look forward to the day when we will be free of all earthly trials and kneel before the throne of Almighty God, where we hope to hear the words, "His lord said to him, 'Well *done*, good and faithful servant; you were faithful over a few things, I will make you ruler over many things. Enter into the joy of your lord'" Matthew 25:21 (NKJV).

Contact Information

Lovebound Ministries

Lovebound Ministries features Janet Crews and Kay Coulter. Since 1985, they have served together in a unique team ministry as conference speaker and praise leader, combining their gifts and callings to communicate a message of hope and encouragment. Presentations include:

Personalities in Perspective

A Scripture-based study of personalities that promotes understanding and harmony in the Body of Christ. Janet and Kay offer a dynamic, inspirational, yet humorous presentation.

Free to Be

Janet and Kay can both testify of God's power to free them from their pasts. In the "Free to Be" conferences, they teach how each woman can experience victory in her life through a loving, growing relationship with Jesus Christ.

Circle of Friends

The Circle of Friends presentation emphasizes the importance of one-on-one relationships and how God uses them in the ministry of reconciliation. Janet Crews and Kay Coulter challenge listeners to see friendships as outreach and discipleship opportunities.

Experiencing God

Janet and Kay present Henry Blackaby's study of the Seven Realities in coming to know and experience God.

For more information on booking conferences or retreats, contact Kay at:

806 Hopi Trail, Temple, TX 76504
or
(800)776-6713
or
www.loveboundministries.com

Other Published Works by B. Kay Coulter

Victim/Victor: It's Your Choice
(Xulon Press 2002)

This book explores the different choices available to us as Christians, and challenges the reader to look to God's Word for healing and practical counsel. For the reader who is still living as a victim, this book will encourage him to look to God for the power to overcome his past, receive healing, and go on to minister to others. The reader will also receive guidance for breaking the cycle of generational abuse. For those in ministry, this book can be a useful tool for helping others who are still in bondage to chronic anger, fear, and bitterness.

To order, contact Xulon Press at 866-381-2665

Proverbs for Personalities
(Goss Publishing 2000)

In *Proverbs for Personalities*, Kay highlights certain Scriptures and then applies them to each personality according to individual traits. These are then divided into two categories: affirmations (pointing to traits that are considered strengths), and admonitions (pointing to traits that are considered weaknesses). Mrs. Coulter says that "through the study of personalities, you can understand yourself and others better, and this results in relationships being enhanced."

To order, contact B. Kay Coulter at
(800)-776-6713

Printed in the United States
18606LVS00002B/1-81